PEGGY PORSCHEN®

A Year in Cake

HOW TO USE THIS BOOK

* Some of the designs in the book refer to recipes and techniques in The Basics chapter (pages 162–181). I recommend that you read each recipe carefully before getting started to ensure that you have all the ingredients and equipment you need. You will also find a useful list of baking and decorating equipment on page 164 and recommended suppliers on page 182.
* Baking times vary from oven to oven. Always check your bake two-thirds of the way through the suggested cooking time and turn your tray or cake tin if the bake seems to be browning unevenly; many ovens have hotspots.
* While caster sugar is widely available in the UK, readers in the US can substitute granulated sugar.
* The eggs in the recipes are given in UK sizes. Readers in the US should go up a size, so a 'medium egg' in the book will be a 'large egg' in the US.

PEGGY PORSCHEN®

A Year in Cake

SEASONAL RECIPES AND DREAMY STYLE SECRETS
FROM THE PRETTIEST BAKERY IN THE WORLD

PHOTOGRAPHY BY PAUL PLEWS

Hardie Grant

QUADRILLE

Contents

The Pursuit of Prettiness

The warming scent of sugar and spice, and the gravitational pull of nature's flora and fauna have always been in my life. As a child growing up in a small village near Cologne in Germany, I simply adored baking cakes. It was a love that was passed to me, along with timeless recipes and know-how, by both my mother and my grandmother. Added to this, my mother was a florist. What could be more idyllic than a beautifully laid table, set with exquisite flowers and rounded off with a lovingly homemade treat? This to me is happiness. In fact, nearly all of my most treasured childhood memories involve a mix of delectable cakes and beautifully themed get-togethers. No matter what else is going on in life, I can still always find solace and a moment of peace in the beauty of the four seasons, played out through something deliciously sweet to taste and equally pleasing to the eye. And sharing this feeling with others is a pursuit I have taken great pleasure from my whole life.

It came as no surprise to my family when I announced my dream to become a cake designer. However, my path to success wasn't mapped out for me. My father, believing that I would find stability in a more traditional profession, encouraged me to keep my passion as a hobby and focus my career efforts elsewhere. It was during this period of soul-searching that I became an air stewardess – having always hugely enjoyed travel – and happened to discover the art of 'British sugarcraft' when on regular trips to London. When I shared my discovery with my father, he said, 'Go for it, but challenge yourself to become one of the best.' Propelled by my longing for a life in pâtisserie, and determined to prove myself, I secured a place on Le Cordon Bleu's 'The Grand Diploma of Cuisine and Pâtisserie' and was overjoyed to graduate in 1999.

Being on the cusp of a new millennium, there was a palpable buzz of excitement and energy in the air. I really believed that anything was possible and threw myself into a prestigious pastry chef role at The Lanesborough hotel, followed by a cake decorating position at celebrated bakers Konditor & Cook. Despite not yet being engaged (that came later, to my husband and business partner Bryn), I was obsessed with wedding magazines and used to buy all the new editions each month. I fell in love with the whimsical themes and was, of course, always desperate to see the cake choice. I happened to stumble across one of the most beautiful cakes I had ever seen, which had been made for Lucy Gemmell, who was founder and director of high-end caterers Rhubarb Food Design. I thought, 'I have to work for this company', and, luckily for me, I did.

Not long after, my first big break came when Rhubarb was hired to cater for Sir Elton John's annual White Tie and Tiara Ball. The creative brief was for an edible Fabergé egg and I took the challenge and ran with it. After days of experimenting, it finally took a team of eight to handmake 14,000 miniature blossoms to decorate 550 eggs, in pearlescent pink and blue. The result was an edible Fabergé egg for each guest, who simply had to pop the gold-crowned lid off and enjoy the pudding inside. The media went wild for the eggs and they featured everywhere. It wasn't long before wedding cake briefs started arriving from A-list celebrities, royals and VIPs, providing me with such incredible experiences that I will never forget.

Riding on the crest of a wave, it was in 2003 that I made the leap to launch my own bespoke cake company. I used everything that I had learnt and threw my heart and soul into making the business work. I ate, slept and breathed cakes and followed my gut instinct to really push boundaries in cake design. However, I always had an underlying longing to share my love of cake more widely, and it was after the 2008 recession that I took my chance to follow a change in direction.

Finally opening the doors to my picture-perfect Peggy Porschen Parlour in London's Belgravia in 2010 was the icing on my cake. I really felt that I had found a home within this quaint neighbourhood made up of independent, artisan boutiques and craftsmen. I couldn't think of a better place to begin sharing my own craft with the world. Finding an identity for the Parlour came naturally, as it was finally an opportunity to share my love of fairy-tale pinks, modern romance and whimsical cake art on a daily basis. The Parlour has represented my pursuit of prettiness since day one and it is instinct that led me to paint the shop front an icing-sugar pink. This hadn't been done before and it could have been polarising, but instead it was magnetic. The Parlour elevated traditional favourites with a grown-up twist and allowed so many local customers and visitors to the area to connect with their inner child. Much like many of the recipes that feature in this book.

Having made the decision to step back from bespoke cake design following the birth of our son Max in 2013, Bryn and I evolved the business to allow a much greater focus on the 'ready-to-eat' Parlour collections and customer experience, whilst also balancing our roles as parents. It was in 2015, in celebration of the RHS Chelsea Flower show, that we created our first floral installation covering the arches of the Parlour. It was such a success and catapulted us onto travel magazine covers, airline advertisement campaigns and social media platforms all over the world. Our pretty pink corner of London became a travel destination in its own right, and it really felt that we had officially 'taken off' as the place to go for cake and design lovers from all over the world.

Seeing the Parlour in this new light, we had the idea of creatively aligning our edible collections with our seasonal installations and from this, one of the most inspiring creative processes was born. In partnership with the wonderful florist and stylist Mathew Dickinson, we carefully select a new creative angle for each season. Working approximately six months ahead, hours and hours of creative planning take place before finally revealing the Parlour's latest installation and cake collection – which is why for this book, it felt so important to share this insight alongside the recipes.

Following the successful opening of our flagship Parlour, Peggy Porschen Chelsea, in 2019 and the signing of this new book (to follow my previous nine titles), we were once again riding a wave of triumph. We did not know what was around the corner and, as for so many businesses, the 2020 Covid pandemic brought much of the hospitality and travel industry to an unexpected standstill. Having grown used to long queues of international customers waiting patiently for a table at our Parlours, and selling out of cupcakes and cakes most weekends, we were suddenly left in the position of having to temporarily close our doors.

Whilst the Peggy Porschen Parlours are eponymous, it is without doubt a joint effort between Bryn and me – we wouldn't be where we are today without either one of us. Therefore, we used 'lockdown' to recalibrate a little and decide what was really important to our business. It was quite simple really when you look back at where we have come from; it is the love of exquisite baking and being able to continually evolve and share this craft in the most beautiful way we can. We have so many plans for the future of Peggy Porschen Cakes and it is our greatest wish that our loyal followers can continue to enjoy this journey with us.

For me, the Peggy Porschen Parlour story has always been one of natural evolution. Born from a passion for what I do, the business is nurtured, developed and loved much like a child. I am fully devoted and have never done anything in a half-hearted way. Whilst perhaps in some sense this perfectionist mindset could be my weakness, it is also my source of strength. I'm naturally drawn to working with people of the same mentality and believe it's crucial to have a creative team to bounce off. It is now with 10 years of the Parlour under our belt that I feel ready to share tips and creative inspiration, so you too can add magic to your seasonal celebrations through, what I see as, the therapeutic art of baking and styling. Enjoy!

With love from Peggy x

Valentine's Day

The rhythm of the seasons is what has come to guide our collection and installation themes at the Parlours. And when it comes to Valentine's Day, this is the seasonal shift that quickens my heartbeat in the best kind of way. As a business built on a love of romance and the arresting power of all things pink and pretty, it is in many ways the season that is most fitting for us. After all, the gift of an exquisitely baked cake as an offering of love is something that transcends generations.

When it comes to creative inspiration, the season of love is a time for us to look through a contemporary lens to work out how we can artistically blend timeless favourites in a way that is applicable to modern love. We've had so many wonderful themes over the years, from La Vie En Rose, which whimsically brought to life Parisian charm, to Sugar Crush, supported by a collaboration with the fabulous Lulu Guinness in honour of her iconic 'lip' handbags.

My favourite of all was our 2020 Love Letters theme. It was all about the handcrafted token of love and a throwback to times when writing letters was one of the most romantic things one could do. We partnered with the beautiful London-based stationery company Martha Brook, to offer baked treats with gift cards. In unison, the Parlour was decked out with pink postboxes and oversized letters hanging in our windows, in honour of some of the greatest loves of all time. For this reason, my favourite recipes in this section are the Love Letter Cookie and the Sealed with a Kiss Cupcake. Whether enjoying the season with a partner, friends or family, I simply cannot imagine a Valentine's Day celebration that doesn't involve sharing lovingly baked treats.

Love Letter Cookies

There is nothing more romantic than expressing your devotion with a love letter. Inspired by our Valentine's installation in 2020, I created this cookie design as a 'token of love', to be (easily) embossed with sweet messages that come from the heart.

MAKES 12 COOKIES

For the cookies

1 quantity Basic Sugar Cookie Dough (see page 165) flavoured with 1 tsp vanilla extract
plain (all-purpose) flour, for dusting

For the decoration

fuchsia pink food colouring paste
1 quantity Half & Half Paste (see page 166)
icing (confectioner's) sugar and cornflour (cornstarch), for dusting
a small amount of white vegetable fat (eg Trex)

pearl edible lustre spray (see Stockists, page 182)
2 tbsp Royal Icing, soft peak consistency (see page 167)

Specialist equipment (see page 164 for a basic equipment list and page 182 for stockists)

envelope cookie cutter set (see Stockists, page 182, or template below and instructions on page 14)
small heart-shaped cutter (2–3cm/¾–1¼in diameter)
'love' and 'love you more' embossers
small piping bag, or make your own paper piping bag (see page 168)

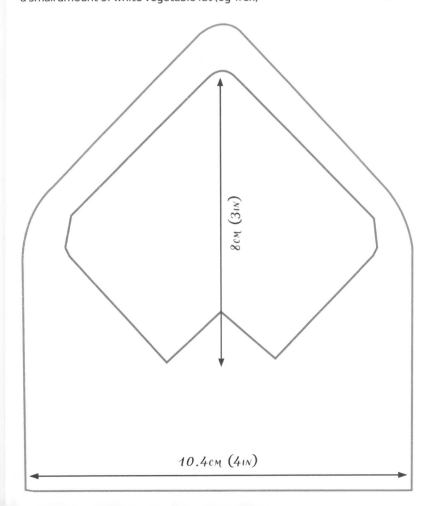

8cm (3in)

10.4cm (4in)

TO BAKE THE COOKIES

Preheat the oven to 175°C fan/375°F/Gas 5 and line 2 baking trays with baking parchment.

To make your own cookie templates, refer to the design on page 13. You will need one template for the open envelope and a separate one for the smaller envelope lining. Trace or photocopy the outlines, glue them onto pieces of card and cut them out.

Unwrap the chilled cookie dough and briefly knead it through to soften it slightly. Place it onto a lightly floured work surface and roll it out to a thickness of about 5mm (¼in).

Using the large open envelope cutter, cut out about 12 cookies. If you've made templates, place them on the cookie dough and cut around them with a kitchen knife to make about 12 cookies. Place them onto the lined baking trays, spaced apart by at least 1cm (½in). Ensure that there are no wrinkles in the paper under the cookies and weigh the edges of the paper down if using a fan-assisted oven, otherwise the cookies may lift up during the baking process and turn out uneven. Put the trays of cookies in the fridge to chill for about 10 minutes.

Bake in the preheated oven for 8–12 minutes, turning the trays once during baking to ensure they bake evenly. When cooked, they should look golden brown and spring back when you press down with your finger. Allow the cookies to cool on the trays.

TO DECORATE THE COOKIES

Following the instructions for colouring on page 166, use fuchsia pink food colouring to colour 240g (8½oz) of the half & half paste to a pastel shade of pink. Wrap both the pink paste and the remaining white paste in cling film until ready to use.

Lightly dust a smooth surface or plastic board with cornflour and place the pastel pink paste on top. Apply a thin layer of vegetable fat to a rolling pin and roll the paste out to a thickness of 1mm (⅟₃₂in).

Using the embossers, press messages ('love' or 'love you more') into the paste, spaced well apart to allow for the envelope lining cutter shapes between

them. Use the envelope lining cutter to cut out the envelope linings with the messages sitting nicely centred. Repeat this step to emboss and cut out 12 pieces in total. Leave them to rest on a smooth surface that has been lightly dusted with icing sugar or cornflour and cover with cling film until needed. Wrap any remaining paste in cling film for later use.

Roll out the white paste to the same 1mm (⅟₃₂in) thickness. Using the large open envelope cookie cutter, stamp out 12 large envelope pieces. Leave them to semi-set on a smooth, dusted surface for 5–10 minutes. Reserve any remaining paste for later use.

Once the white envelopes are slightly set, take the envelope lining cutter and cut out the spaces into which you will later insert the pink paste cutouts. Be careful not to stretch the envelope shapes.

Unwrap the pink paste cutouts and lightly spray them with the edible lustre spray until they have a shimmer and look like pearlised tissue paper.

Carefully insert the pink paste cutouts into the white envelopes. Adjust and push the paste colours into position while still soft to ensure that there are no gaps between the pink and the white paste.

Mix about 1 tbsp royal icing with 1 tsp water to make a sugar glue. Brush the top of the cookies, a few at a time, thinly with the sugar glue. Carefully slide a large palette knife underneath a white and pink envelope sugar paste set, lift and place on top of the cookies. Press the paste onto the cookie while it is still slightly pliable to ensure there are no gaps between the cookie and the paste. Repeat with the rest of the cookies.

Mix the leftover half & half paste with a little more pink food colour to a bright shade of pink. Roll out the paste to about the thickness of a ruler and stamp out one heart shape per cookie.

Put the remaining royal icing into a small piping bag and snip a small tip off the bottom. Use it to trace the outlines of the envelope sections.

Stick a heart into the middle of each cookie and leave until the royal icing has dried completely.

Sealed with a Kiss
CHOCOLATE & RASPBERRY CUPCAKES

A match made in heaven, this cupcake is a firm favourite in our Valentine's Day line-up. The chocolate sponge is rich and smooth, while the raspberry meringue buttercream is elegant and light. In the middle is a hidden core of raspberry jam bursting with fruitiness, perfectly balancing the richness of the chocolate and the sweetness of the buttercream. Finished with a simple, yet striking handmade sugar wax seal, this cupcake wins hearts every time.

MAKES 24 CUPCAKES

For the sugar wax seals

150g (5oz) Half & Half Paste (made from 75g/2½oz sugar paste and 75g/2½oz sugar florist paste, see page 166)
claret red food colouring paste (see Stockists, page 182)
a small amount of white vegetable fat (eg Trex)
pearl edible lustre spray (see Stockists, page 182)

For the chocolate cupcakes

105g (3½oz/7 tbsp) unsalted butter, softened
285g (10oz/1½ cups less 1 tbsp) light brown sugar
125g (4½oz) dark chocolate (53% cocoa solids), chopped or in buttons
165ml (5¼fl oz/⅔ cup) whole milk
2 large eggs
180g (6¼oz/1⅓ cups) plain (all-purpose) flour
½ tsp baking powder
½ tsp bicarbonate of soda (baking soda)
pinch of salt
1 tbsp cocoa powder

For the raspberry filling

120g (4¼oz/1 cup) fresh raspberries
100g (3½oz/⅓ cup) good-quality raspberry jam

For the raspberry meringue buttercream

125g (4½oz/½ cup) Raspberry Purée (see page 179), made from 250g (8¾oz/2¼ cups) fresh or frozen raspberries, cooled
1 cupcake quantity Meringue Buttercream (see page 176)

For the decoration

24 fresh raspberries
24 freeze-dried edible rose petals (see Stockists, page 182)
small pink sugar pearls (see Stockists, page 182)

Specialist equipment (see page 164 for a basic equipment list and page 182 for stockists)

rose wax seal stamp
2 x 12-hole cupcake tray
24 red paper baking cases
large piping bag fitted with large narrow-toothed star nozzle

TO MAKE THE SUGAR WAX SEALS

Following the instructions for colouring on page 166, use a small amount of claret red food colouring to colour the half & half paste to a pastel pink. Wrap the paste in cling film and rest for about 10 minutes to allow it to firm up slightly.

Roll the paste into a sausage about 1cm (½in) thick, then cut it into 1cm- (½in-) wide pieces using a kitchen knife.

Roll each piece into a ball between your fingers, using a small amount of vegetable fat to keep the paste smooth.

Rub some more vegetable fat thinly over the metal embosser plate of the rose wax seal stamp, as well as on the work surface.

Place a ball on the work surface and evenly press the embosser into the paste until you can see the paste showing around the edges of the embosser. Lift the stamp to reveal the sugar wax seal. Repeat to make 24 sugar wax seals.

Spray the wax seals with the pearl edible lustre and let them dry. They will last for several days if stored in a dry place, so you can make them ahead of time if you prefer.

TO MAKE THE CHOCOLATE CUPCAKES

Preheat the oven to 160°C fan/350°F/Gas 4 and line the cupcake trays with the baking cases.

Put the butter and half of the sugar into the bowl of an electric mixer fitted with a paddle attachment and cream together until pale and fluffy. This will take a while, so do this as a first step to allow plenty of time to aerate the mixture.

Put the chocolate, milk and the remaining sugar into a small saucepan on a low heat and bring to a light simmer, stirring occasionally to ensure the chocolate doesn't burn.

Beat the eggs in a separate bowl, then slowly add them to the butter and sugar mixture, mixing at low speed all the time.

Sift together the flour, baking powder, bicarbonate of soda, salt and cocoa powder. Add this to the butter and sugar mixture in 2 batches, still mixing at low speed and waiting until the first batch is combined before adding the next.

Once the chocolate has melted and the milk has come to a light simmer, remove the pan from the heat and slowly pour the hot chocolate milk into the batter while still mixing at low speed. Be careful not to splash yourself with any hot mixture. Scrape the bottom of the mixing bowl with a rubber spatula to ensure that everything is well combined.

Transfer the chocolate batter to a large jug and pour the mix into the baking cases, filling each one two-thirds full.

Immediately transfer the trays to the preheated oven while the batter is still warm and bake for 15–20 minutes, depending on your oven.

The cupcakes are cooked when the tops spring back to the touch and the edges of the baking cases have shrunk away from the sides of the baking tray. The texture should be soft and slightly sticky, so if inserting a knife to test if cooked, there should be a small amount of crumb sticking to the blade.

Remove from the oven and leave to rest in the cupcake trays for a few minutes.

Transfer the cupcakes to a wire rack and leave to cool completely.

When cool, chill for about 30 minutes to firm the sponge up a little.

TO MAKE THE RASPBERRY FILLING

Place the fresh raspberries in a small saucepan with 1 tbsp water and cook until they are soft and falling apart.

Crush them using a fork until they form a purée. The texture should be thick, so if the purée is still runny, carry on cooking until the liquid has reduced down a little.

Allow to cool completely.

Once cool, add the jam to the cooked raspberries and mix together. Cover with cling film and set aside to fill the cupcakes later.

TO MAKE THE RASPBERRY MERINGUE BUTTERCREAM

Slowly add the cooled raspberry purée to the meringue buttercream and mix until well combined. Ensure that the purée and buttercream are at the same room temperature to prevent the mixture from splitting.

TO FILL AND DECORATE THE CUPCAKES

Scoop a small well out of the centre of each cupcake using a melon baller.

Using a teaspoon, fill the centres of the cakes with the raspberry filling you made earlier.

Fill a piping bag fitted with a large narrow-toothed star nozzle with the raspberry meringue buttercream. Pipe a generous rosette of buttercream on top of each cupcake.

While the buttercream is still soft, place a fresh raspberry on top, as well as a rose petal, a sugar wax seal and a sprinkle of pink sugar pearls.

Serve as soon as possible, or chill for about 30 minutes until the buttercream has slightly set before transporting them. Always serve and enjoy at room temperature. The sugar wax seals may melt if exposed to humidity and should be consumed within 24 hours once placed on a cupcake.

VALENTINE'S DAY STYLE SECRETS

In my eyes, wreaths are not just for Christmas and are a lovely way to connect with the seasons throughout the year. For Valentine's Day, a simple heart-shaped floral wreath hung in your window with a lush pink satin ribbon will make a lovely detail in your home. To really impress your loved one, a skilled calligrapher will be able to inscribe a love message, or the names of you and your sweetheart, on a thick paper banner, which you can attach centrally across your hanging heart.

♡

To bring to life the 'Love Letters' theme mentioned in this chapter, small pink letterboxes can be hired. A good source of traders for this can be found in the wedding industry. Silk roses are a good investment if you plan to style your home quite often. Unlike fresh flowers, they will last for as long as you need, and you can use them time and time again. It's a growing market, and well worth looking at the suppliers I have given. To complete the letterbox look, arrange the silk roses as if cascading out of the letterbox.

♡

For beautiful pastel pink and white stationery, I highly recommend looking at Martha Brook, which also offers calligraphy workshops. I took one myself and was surprised how quickly I was able to learn simple yet effective writing techniques. It's become a wonderful skill for writing special cards and gift tags.

♡

Complete the look by decorating your floral letterbox with pretty envelopes, and writing well known love poems and quotes onto pieces of paper. You can also find beautiful sugar wax seal stamps online, with roses, hearts and initials. These extra-special finishing touches always have such a wonderful impact.

Heart to Heart

STRAWBERRY & MARC DE CHAMPAGNE CAKE

This beautiful cake design is proof that baking is love. Setting a passionate tone, an ombre pink and ivory buttercream creates an eye-catching backdrop for a 'shout it from the rooftops' celebration with sprinkles and handmade sugar hearts. Just as beautiful on the inside, a delicious vanilla sponge is layered with strawberry and Marc de Champagne buttercream.

MAKES A 15CM (6IN) CAKE (SERVES 10)

For the heart decorations

50g (2oz) Half & Half Paste (made from 25g/1oz sugar paste and 25g/1oz sugar florist paste, see page 166)
fuchsia pink food colouring paste (see Stockists, page 182)
a small amount of white vegetable fat (eg Trex)

For the Marc de Champagne sugar syrup

150g (5½oz/¾ cup) caster sugar
150ml (5fl oz/scant ⅔ cup) water
1 tbsp Marc de Champagne (optional, contains alcohol) or 1 tsp vanilla extract

For the vanilla sponge

200g (7oz/¾ cup plus 2 tbsp) unsalted butter, softened
pinch of salt
200g (7oz/1 cup) caster sugar
1 tsp vanilla extract
4 medium eggs, at room temperature
200g (7oz/1½ cups) self-raising flour, sifted

For the strawberry and Marc de Champagne meringue buttercream

80g (2¾oz) Strawberry Purée (see page 179) made from about 160g (5½oz/1⅓ cups) fresh strawberries, cooled
about 2 tbsp Marc de Champagne (optional, contains alcohol) or 1 tsp vanilla extract
1 layer cake quantity Meringue Buttercream (see page 176)

For the sprinkles mix

pink and red glimmer sugar hearts (see Stockists, page 182)
matt 100s and 1000s red and pink mix (see Stockists, page 182)
silver metallic sugar pearls (see Stockists, page 182)
metallic macaroni rods (see Stockists, page 182)

Specialist equipment (see page 164 for a basic equipment list and page 182 for stockists)

silicone heart sugar mould (heart should have a diameter of about 1.5cm/½in)
3 x 15cm (6in) shallow cake tins
15cm (6in) thin cake board
large piping bag
round piping nozzle (optional) and star piping nozzle

TO MAKE THE HEART DECORATIONS

Following the instructions for colouring on page 166, use pink food colouring to colour the half & half paste to a light shade of pink. Wrap the paste in cling film and rest for about 10 minutes to allow it to firm up slightly.

Lightly grease the heart silicone mould with the vegetable fat.

Roll the paste into a sausage and cut off 3 hazelnut-sized pieces.

Roll a piece into a ball and press it into the heart mould. Flatten the back and trim off any excess paste.

To release the sugar heart, bend the mould outward until the heart drops out and let it set. Repeat to make 3 pale pink hearts.

Now add a touch more pink food colouring to the remaining paste to make a medium shade of pink. Repeat the instructions above to make 3 further hearts in this shade of pink.

Finally, add a touch more colouring to the remaining paste for a dark pink and make a final 4 hearts as above.

You can make the hearts well in advance as they last for days if stored in a dry place at room temperature.

TO MAKE THE MARC DE CHAMPAGNE SUGAR SYRUP

Put the sugar and water in a saucepan, bring to a boil and cook until the sugar is dissolved. Remove from the heat and allow to cool.

Once cool, add the Marc de Champagne, if using, or the vanilla extract.

TO MAKE THE SPONGE LAYERS

Preheat the oven to 175°C fan/375°F/Gas 5. Grease 3 x 15cm (6in) shallow cake tins with oil spray and line the bases with baking parchment.

Put the butter, salt, sugar and vanilla extract into the bowl of an electric mixer fitted with a paddle attachment and beat at medium–high speed until pale and fluffy.

In another bowl, lightly beat the eggs, then slowly pour them into the butter and sugar mix while beating on medium speed. Watch as the eggs combine with the butter mix and stop pouring if the batter needs time to come together, then add more. The eggs and butter should both be at room temperature to avoid splitting. However, should the mixture split, add 1 tbsp flour to bring the batter back together before adding more egg.

Once all the eggs are incorporated, fold in the flour in 2 batches, gently combining each time. Scrape the bottom of the bowl using a rubber spatula to ensure the batter is evenly mixed.

Divide the batter evenly between the 3 prepared cake tins and gently spread the batter towards the edges. It should be slightly higher around the sides with a slight dip in the middle; this will ensure that it bakes evenly when it rises.

Bake in the preheated oven for 20–30 minutes. The sponges are cooked when the edges come away from the sides of the cake tin and the tops spring back to the touch. To test if cooked, insert a knife or wooden skewer into the sponge: it should come out clean.

Leave the sponges to rest in the tins for about 10–15 minutes and brush the tops with the sugar syrup. This will prevent the cakes from forming a hard crust and the heat will ensure that the moisture and flavour are absorbed evenly. Reserve the remainder of the syrup for layering.

Once slightly cooled, unmould the sponges from the cake tins carefully without breaking the edges – use a small kitchen knife to release the sides if required. Leave to cool completely on a wire rack.

The sponges can be baked a day in advance. To store overnight, wrap them in cling film or kitchen foil and store in the fridge.

TO MAKE THE STRAWBERRY AND MARC DE CHAMPAGNE MERINGUE BUTTERCREAM

Combine the cooled strawberry purée with the Marc de Champagne, if using, or the vanilla extract.

Transfer one-third of the meringue buttercream to a separate bowl and set aside.

Slowly fold in the strawberry and Marc de Champagne purée through the remaining two-thirds of the buttercream and gently mix until well combined. Ensure that the purée and buttercream are at the same room temperature to prevent the mixture from splitting.

TO ASSEMBLE AND DECORATE THE CAKE

Layer and crumb coat the sponge layers using the strawberry meringue buttercream and the Marc de Champagne sugar syrup, as per the instructions on page 172.

Divide the remaining strawberry buttercream into 2 equal portions. Mix one half with a small amount of fuchsia pink food colouring to a bright pink shade. You may wish to add a tiny bit of pink food colour to the pale pink buttercream as well to give it a little bit of a lift.

Once the crumb coat has set, place the cake back on the turntable and cover the top evenly with plain buttercream using a palette knife.

See step-by-step pictures on pages 26 and 27 for the following instructions.

Apply 3 evenly-sized rings of dark pink, pale pink and plain buttercream around the sides, using a palette knife. (Alternatively, you can spoon each colour into a piping bag fitted with a round nozzle and pipe rings around the sides.)

Start at the bottom layer and spread the dark pink buttercream one-third of the way up the side of the cake. Follow suit with the pale pink buttercream for the middle third and finish with the plain buttercream for the upper third and the top of the cake. Reserve any remaining plain buttercream to pipe the rosettes later.

Smooth all 3 buttercream stripes using a side scraper. If not smooth after the first time, wipe the edge of the side scraper clean and go around again and again, until the sides look smooth. This time there should be no cake crumb visible.

Clean up the top edge of the cake by spreading the overhanging buttercream from the edge towards the middle of the cake using a palette knife or side scraper. Transfer the cake to a cake board and chill again for about 1 hour.

Place all your sugar sprinkles in a bowl and mix them up.

Cut a piece of baking parchment that is a few inches wider than the cake top. Take the cold cake straight from the fridge and place the baking parchment on top. Place a cake disc (or the loose base of a larger cake tin) over the baking parchment to support the cake, then carefully and swiftly flip the cake over so that it's upside down.

Press the sprinkle mix around the top edge of the cake (which is now facing down) with your hands. Doing this while the cake is sitting upside down on a flat surface will ensure a clean sharp edge around the top of the cake.

Turn the cake back over, discard the cake disc and stick a few macaroni rods around the sides using a pair of tweezers. Peel the baking parchment off the top of the cake.

Spoon the remaining plain buttercream into a piping bag with a star nozzle attachment. You may want to gently mix it through before filling it into the bag to ensure no lumps have formed while you were decorating the cake.

Pipe 10 evenly-sized and -spaced out rosettes around the top of the cake using the plain buttercream.

Stick a sugar heart on top of each rosette, alternating the colours, and sprinkle with a small amount of sugar sprinkles.

Spring & Easter

As welcome as the dawn chorus, the spring awakening is my favourite season at the Parlour. London becomes alive with an explosion of delicate blossoms and buds that pulls us from our winter hibernation and steers us, as if spellbound, to the many parks and pretty neighbourhoods that the city offers. Our Parlours are always in harmony with this early-blooming floral symphony and the annual launch of our spring collection and installation never fails to provide a rush of joy that takes me right back to childhood.

We always celebrate Mother's Day (in the UK this falls in March) followed by Easter at the Parlours. There's a wonderful buzz and palpable air of excitement as families gather to mark the occasions or buy gifts for loved ones.

This has always been my favourite time of year to travel home and spend time with my family in Germany. Easter is celebrated with a beautifully laid and decorated breakfast table, dotted with coloured eggs and an Easter brioche loaf to tuck into, before the children impatiently rush into the garden to enjoy an Easter egg hunt.

From the sweetest Vegan Jam Heart Cookies for Mother's Day to the easy-to-follow Easter Meringue Nests and the elegant Easter Speckled Nests Vanilla Chiffon Cake, which will make a beautiful centrepiece on your festive table, these recipes really are full of the joys of spring.

Chirpy Chick Cookies

This adorable character cookie is full of the joys of spring. It may look a little tricky to decorate, but the hand painting technique is easier than you think. I will carefully guide you with my step-by-step images and instructions to ensure you achieve an artistic result to be proud of. This is also a great recipe to get the kids involved with and let them create their own little springtime characters.

MAKES 12 CHICK COOKIES

For the vanilla cookies

1 quantity Basic Sugar Cookie Dough (see page 165) flavoured with 1 tsp vanilla extract
plain (all-purpose) flour, for dusting

For the decoration

1 quantity Half & Half Paste (see page 166)
icing (confectioner's) sugar and cornflour (cornstarch), for dusting
a small amount of white vegetable fat (eg Trex)
yellow, pink, peppermint green and black food colouring pastes

a small amount of clear alcohol, such as vodka (alternatively use lemon juice)
fine tip black edible food pen (see Stockists, page 182)
2 tbsp Royal Icing, soft peak consistency (see page 167)
edible blush pink blossom tint (see Stockists, page 182)

Specialist equipment (see page 164 for a basic equipment list and page 182 for stockists)

Easter chick cookie cutter
small piping bag, or make your own paper piping bag (see page 168)

TO BAKE THE COOKIES

Preheat the oven to 175°C fan/375°F/Gas 5 and line 2 baking trays with baking parchment.

Unwrap the chilled cookie dough and briefly knead it through to soften it slightly.

Place the dough onto a lightly floured work surface and roll it out to an even thickness of about 5mm (¼in).

Using the chick cookie cutter, stamp out 12 cookies and place them onto the lined baking trays, spaced apart by at least 1cm (½in). Ensure that there are no wrinkles in the paper under the cookies and weigh the edges of the paper down if using a fan-assisted oven, otherwise the cookies may lift up during the baking process and turn out uneven. Put the trays of cookies in the fridge to chill for about 10 minutes.

Bake in the preheated oven for 8–12 minutes, turning the trays once during baking to ensure they bake evenly. When cooked, they should look golden brown and spring back when pressing down with your finger. Allow the cookies to cool on the trays.

TO DECORATE THE COOKIES

Lightly dust a smooth surface or plastic board with cornflour and place the half & half paste on top. Apply a thin layer of vegetable fat to a rolling pin and roll the paste out to a thickness of 1mm (¹⁄₃₂in).

Using the chick cookie cutter, stamp out 12 pieces (plus a few extra to test the painting technique). Leave them to semi-set on a smooth surface that has been lightly dusted with icing sugar or cornflour.

Prepare your paint colours; you will need yellow, peach (by mixing pink and yellow), peppermint green and black. Put a small amount of each paste colour into a well of a colour mixing palette. Add a

drop of the clear alcohol and dilute each colour to a runny, ink-like consistency. Test the colours on the spare chick cutouts – if too dark, add a little more alcohol, if too light, add more colour.

Once the chick sugar cutouts have formed a dry skin, paint the peachy-yellow tulip petals using a flat artist's brush. Start with yellow as the base colour, painting from the bottom of the chick up to the tip of each petal. Use long, even strokes and go over each petal as many times as you need to until the colour evenly covers each petal.

While still wet, add strokes of the peach colour to the petals to create graduating shades – the colours should nicely blend together. Try to avoid getting drips or splashes of colour on the paste. The alcohol will eventually evaporate and the colours will completely dry after a while, however, if the icing gets too wet, the colours can melt the sugar paste or mark the surface.

Paint the pastel green leaves following the same technique and let dry. Ensure you clean the brushes thoroughly before using a new colour.

Mix 1 tbsp royal icing with 1 tsp water to form a sugar glue and brush it over the cookies, a few at a time.

Stick a painted chick cutout on top of each cookie (they should still be slightly pliable) and gently press down around the edges. Let the paste dry completely (this is important before you apply the black paint as this can bleed into the paste if still soft. If you are an experienced cookie painter, you can ice your cookies first and paint all once dry, however I find that accidents happen and you may lose a few cookies this way).

Trace the eyes and little head feathers using the edible food pen.

Using a fine, thin round artist's brush, paint over the head feathers and eyelids with the black food colouring and add the lashes. I recommend practising this on some spare chick cutouts before painting directly onto the final chicks, as the eyes are the trickiest part and require steady hands and the right colour consistency.

Outline the leaves and petals using the black food colouring. (Note: Black takes longer to dry than other food colours. To avoid smudging, allow plenty of time for it to dry and be careful when handling the cookies.)

Using a clean and dry round artist's brush and the blush pink blossom tint, give the chicks pink cheeks underneath the eyelids. Dip the brush into the blossom tint, then dab it off on a paper towel before applying it onto the icing.

To pipe the yellow beak, mix the remaining royal icing with a tiny bit of yellow food colouring paste and a small amount of water to a pale yellow icing that is slightly softer than soft peak consistency, but not quite runny. Spoon it into a small piping bag and snip a small tip off the end. Pipe a triangular shaped beak between the eyes of all the chicks.

Fill the beak outlines with the yellow icing and increase the pressure when squeezing the icing out of the bag. This way you should get a smooth slightly raised beak shape.

Leave the cookies to set until the royal icing and food colours have dried completely. Should the black colour still remain wet once the rest of the cookie has dried, you can absorb some of the liquid by carefully pressing a sheet of paper towel on top.

The cookies make lovely gifts if wrapped in cellophane bags (you can get biodegradable ones online) and can be stored in an airtight contrainer for up to 6 weeks.

Spring Tulip
STRAWBERRY & RHUBARB CUPCAKES

This seasonally sweet cupcake, with a hand painted pink tulip decoration, is a delightful way to celebrate the arrival of spring. Classic vanilla sponge is filled with rhubarb and strawberry preserve and topped with an artful swirl of strawberry meringue buttercream.

MAKES 24 CUPCAKES

For the sugar tulip decorations

80g (2¾oz) Half & Half Paste (made from 40g/1½oz sugar paste and 40g/1½oz sugar florist paste, see page 166)
icing (confectioner's) sugar and cornflour (cornstarch), for dusting
a small amount of white vegetable fat (eg Trex)
fuchsia pink, peppermint green and black food colouring pastes (see Stockists, page 182)
clear alcohol, such as vodka (alternatively use lemon juice)

For the vanilla sugar syrup

150g (5½oz/¾ cup) caster sugar
150ml (5fl oz/scant ⅔ cup) water
1 tsp vanilla extract

For the vanilla cupcakes

225g (8oz/1 cup) unsalted butter, softened
225g (8oz/1 cup plus 2 tbsp) caster sugar
pinch of salt
1 tsp vanilla extract
4 medium eggs
225g (8oz/1¾ cups) self-raising flour, sifted

For the rhubarb and strawberry jam

120g (4¼oz) fresh or frozen rhubarb
80g (2¾oz) fresh or frozen strawberries
140g (5oz/¾ cup less 2 tsp) caster sugar
¼ tsp pectin

For the strawberry meringue buttercream

125g (4½oz) Strawberry Purée (see page 179), made from 250g/9oz fresh strawberries, cooled
1 cupcake quantity Meringue Buttercream (see page 176)
fuchsia pink food colouring paste

For the cupcake decorations

small pink glimmer pearls (see Stockists, page 182)

Specialist equipment (see page 164 for a basic equipment list and page 182 for stockists)

mini tulip cutter
24 rose gold metallic baking cases
2 x 12-hole cupcake baking trays
large piping bag
large piping bag fitted with a large star nozzle

TO MAKE THE TULIP DECORATIONS

Lightly dust a smooth surface or plastic board with cornflour and place the half & half paste on top. Apply a thin layer of vegetable fat to a small rolling pin and roll the paste out to a thickness of 1mm (⅟₃₂in).

Using the mini tulip cutter, stamp out 24–30 tulips (to allow extra for testing and breakages). Place them on a smooth surface that has been lightly dusted with icing sugar or cornflour and allow them to dry completely.

Once the tulips are dry, mix the fuchsia pink and the peppermint green food colour pastes each with a small amount of vodka to a runny ink-like consistency.

Using a soft medium-sized artist's brush, paint the pink petals of all the tulips first and let them dry. Try to achieve different shades of pink for a pretty watercolour effect.

Paint the stems and leaves with the green colouring and let them dry.

Mix the black food colouring with a drop of vodka to a slightly thicker consistency. Using a very fine artist's brush, paint the stems and outline the leaves and petals of each tulip. Let dry. (Note: Black takes longer to dry than other food colours. To avoid smudging, allow plenty of time for it to dry and be careful when handling the cookies.)

TO MAKE THE VANILLA SUGAR SYRUP

Put the sugar, water and vanilla extract in a small saucepan and bring to a boil until the sugar has dissolved. Allow to cool.

TO MAKE THE VANILLA CUPCAKES

Preheat the oven to 175°C fan/375°F/Gas 5 and line the cupcake trays with the baking cases.

Put the butter, sugar, salt and vanilla extract in the bowl of an electric mixer fitted with a paddle attachment and cream together at medium-high speed until pale and fluffy.

Break the eggs into a measuring jug, beat a little, and slowly pour them into the butter mix in a steady stream, mixing at low speed all the time. Watch as the mixture slowly absorbs the eggs. Should it start to split, add 1 tbsp flour to bring it back together, then continue adding the eggs until they are all incorporated.

Add the flour to the batter in 2 batches, still mixing at low speed and waiting until the first batch is combined before adding the next. Scrape the bottom of the mixing bowl with a rubber spatula to ensure that everything is well combined.

Fill a large piping bag with the batter and snip 2.5cm (1in) off the tip. Pipe the batter into the baking cases, filling each one about two-thirds full. Start in the centre of the base of the case, then move the piping bag up and around the outside of the case, leaving a dip in the middle; this will ensure that the cupcakes rise more evenly. Tap the tray down a couple of times on the work surface and leave to rest for 10 minutes before baking them (I find that this prevents the cupcakes from rising too high and cracking open at the top during the baking process).

Bake in the preheated oven for 12–15 minutes. The cupcakes are cooked when they are golden, the tops spring back to the touch and the edges of the baking cases have shrunk away from the sides of the baking tray.

Remove from the oven and leave to rest in the cupcake trays for a few minutes.

Brush the tops of the cakes with the vanilla sugar syrup while still hot. This will ensure the sponges absorb the moisture and prevent a dry crust from forming.

Transfer the cupcakes to a wire rack and leave to cool completely. Wipe the bottoms with a damp cloth if sticky from the syrup. Do not leave the cupcakes to cool in the cupcake tray, as the cases may stick to the bottom of it.

When cool, chill in the fridge for about 30 minutes to slightly firm up the sponge.

TO MAKE THE RHUBARB AND STRAWBERRY JAM

Put the rhubarb, strawberries and 1 tbsp water in a saucepan and cook over a gentle heat until soft and mushy.

Blitz with a stick blender until smooth.

Leave the mixture to cool to 50°C/122°F.

In a small bowl, mix 20g (¾oz/2½ tbsp) of the sugar and the pectin together well until completely combined, then add it to the purée and bring to the boil with a sugar thermometer inside.

Add the remaining sugar and keep cooking, whisking constantly, until the thermometer reaches 103°C/217°F.

Pour into a heatproof bowl and cover with cling film. Allow to cool, then store in the fridge until later use.

TO MAKE THE STRAWBERRY MERINGUE BUTTERCREAM

Carefully whisk the cooled strawberry purée into the meringue buttercream. Ensure that the purée and buttercream are at the same room temperature to prevent the mixture from splitting.

Mix 1 tbsp of the buttercream with some fuchsia food colouring to a bright pink shade, taking care to break down the colour specks with a palette knife.

Mix the coloured buttercream back into the main batch a little at a time, until you achieve a pretty pastel pink colour.

TO ICE AND DECORATE THE CUPCAKES

Scoop a small well out of the centre of each cupcake using a melon baller.

Using a teaspoon, fill the centres of the cakes with the strawberry and rhubarb jam.

Put the strawberry meringue buttercream into a large piping bag fitted with a large star nozzle. Pipe a generous rosette of buttercream on top of each cupcake.

While the buttercream is still soft, place a sugar tulip on top and sprinkle with the pink glimmer pearls.

Serve as soon as possible or chill for about 30 minutes until the buttercream has slightly set before transporting them. Always serve and enjoy at room temperature. The sugar tulips can melt if exposed to humidity and should be consumed within 24 hours once placed on a cupcake.

Easter Meringue Nests

Let the Easter egg hunt begin with my playful twist on a much-loved classic. Soft pink meringue encases a crunchy chocolate egg nest, carefully cushioning a collection of colourful mini chocolate eggs and sugar blossom. For baking pros or baking novices, the recipe provides the option of making or buying pre-made sugar blossoms.

MAKES 10 MERINGUE NESTS

For the sugar blossom decorations (if making your own)

50g (1¾oz) white sugar florist paste
a small amount of white vegetable fat (eg Trex)
pink or purple and yellow food colouring pastes
icing (confectioner's) sugar and cornflour (cornstarch), for dusting
1 heaped tsp Royal Icing (see page 167)

For the meringue nests

300g (10½oz) egg whites (from approx. 10 eggs)
300g (10½oz/1½ cups) caster sugar
300g (10½oz/2 cups plus 2 tbsp) icing (confectioner's) sugar
1½ tsp vanilla extract
pink food colouring paste
1 heaped tsp cocoa powder
1 tsp hot water

For the chocolate crunch filling and decoration

200g (7oz) dark chocolate (53% cocoa solids)
10g (⅓oz) cocoa butter
100g (3½oz/4 cups) cornflakes
about 30 speckled chocolate quails' eggs in various colours
about 20 small speckled milk chocolate eggs in various colours
10 pastel-coloured mini sugar blossoms (if not making your own)

Specialist equipment (see page 164 for a basic equipment list and page 182 for stockists)

primrose blossom cutter and veiner set
small piping bag, or make your own paper piping bag (see page 168)
large piping bag fitted with a large star nozzle

TO MAKE THE SUGAR BLOSSOM DECORATIONS

Mix the sugar florist paste with a small amount of white vegetable fat and knead it through until smooth and pliable. Add a drop of pink or purple food colouring and mix to a pastel shade.

Lightly dust a smooth surface or plastic board with cornflour and place the sugar florist paste on top. Apply a thin layer of vegetable fat to a small rolling pin and roll the paste out to a thickness of 1mm (1/32in).

Using the primrose blossom cutter, stamp out about 10 blossom shapes (plus a few extra in case of breakages). Emboss the soft sugar blossom shapes with the lightly greased blossom silicone veiner. Place each blossom into the well of a colour mixing palette dusted with icing sugar or cornflour and let them dry in a cup shape.

Mix the royal icing with a small amount of yellow food colouring and a drop of water to achieve a pastel yellow icing of soft peak piping consistency (see page 167 for detailed instructions on colouring royal icing and consistencies).

Spoon the icing into a small paper piping bag and snip a small tip off the end.

Pipe 3 small dots into the middle of each blossom, then leave them to dry.

TO MAKE THE MERINGUE NESTS

Preheat the oven to 80°C/210°F/Gas ¼. Draw 10 circles with a diameter of 12cm (4½in) on a sheet of baking parchment and place it upside down on a baking tray.

Put the egg whites and sugar into a metal or glass heatproof bowl and whisk together. Place the bowl over a hot water bath (bain marie) and continue whisking until the meringue becomes white and fluffy and it reaches 55°C/131°F on a sugar thermometer.

Once the temperature is reached, transfer to the bowl of an electric mixer fitted with a whisk attachment and whisk at medium speed until cool.

Once the meringue is cool, gradually add the icing sugar and continue whisking until fully combined and stiff. Add the vanilla extract.

Mix about 1 tbsp of the meringue with a drop of pink food colour and blend together with a palette knife until all the colour specks have dispersed. Little by little, add the coloured meringue back into the white batch and mix until you get an even pastel pink colour.

Spoon the pink meringue into a large piping bag fitted with a large open star nozzle. Only fill the bag about two-thirds full (you can top up the bag later if you have meringue left) and twist the open end of the bag to prevent the meringue from oozing out.

Pipe meringue nests onto the prepared baking tray, using the circles as a size guide. Leave about 5cm (2in) of space between the nests to give them room for spreading. Start piping from the middle of the circle, creating a spiral until you reach the required size, then pipe a ring on top around the outside to form the wall of the nest.

Bake in the preheated oven for about 2 hours, or until the meringues can be lifted clean off the tray. Allow to cool.

Once cool, combine the cocoa powder and hot water. Dip a pastry brush or flat artist's brush into the liquid cocoa, hold it over the meringues and flick the cocoa off with your fingers until the meringues are speckled.

TO MAKE THE CHOCOLATE CRUNCH FILLING AND DECORATE THE NESTS

Melt the chocolate and cocoa butter separately, then mix them together in a large bowl.

Add the cornflakes and mix until completely coated with the chocolate.

Spoon about 1 heaped tbsp of the chocolate crunch filling into each meringue nest. Decorate with the speckled eggs and sugar blossoms while the chocolate is still wet.

Easter Speckled Nests

VANILLA CHIFFON CAKE

The perfect centrepiece for any springtime feast, this wonderfully light and fluffy vanilla chiffon sponge is layered and masked with meringue buttercream. Dressed for Easter in 'Peggy pink' speckled meringue buttercream and crowned with mini chocolate egg nests, this recipe is a real showstopper.

MAKES A 15CM (6IN) CAKE (SERVES 10)

1 quantity Chiffon Sponge (3 x 15cm/6in cakes, see page 171) flavoured with 1 tsp vanilla extract

For the chocolate nests

100g (3½oz) dark chocolate (53% cocoa solids)
1 tsp cocoa butter
50g (1¾oz/2 cups) cornflakes
10 mini chocolate eggs
small pink glimmer pearls (see Stockists, page 182)
10 pastel-coloured mini sugar blossoms (store-bought or make your own, see Easter Meringue Nests recipe on page 38)

For the vanilla meringue buttercream

1 layer cake quantity Meringue Buttercream (see page 176)
1 tsp vanilla extract
fuchsia pink food colouring paste

To decorate the cake

1 tbsp cocoa powder
1 tbsp hot water

Specialist equipment (see page 164 for a basic equipment list and page 182 for stockists)

3 x 15cm (6in) shallow cake tins
15cm (6in) thin cake board
15-hole silicone half-sphere mould (each half sphere 5cm/2in in diameter)

TO MAKE THE CHOCOLATE NESTS

To make the nests, melt the chocolate and cocoa butter separately, then mix together in a large bowl.

Add the cornflakes and mix well until they are completely coated with chocolate.

Spoon a heaped tsp of cornflake mix into each of the half spheres of the silicone tray. While the chocolate is still wet, push one chocolate egg and one blossom into each nest and finish with a sprinkle of glimmer pearls on top.

Chill for a few minutes until set, then unmould and chill again until needed.

TO MAKE THE VANILLA MERINGUE BUTTERCREAM

Stir the vanilla extract into the meringue buttercream.

Mix 1 tbsp of the buttercream with a small amount of fuchsia pink food colouring to a bright pink shade and blend together with a palette knife until all the colour specks have dispersed.

Little by little, add the pink buttercream back to the main batch and mix until you have reached a pretty pastel pink.

TO ASSEMBLE AND DECORATE THE CAKE

Layer and crumb coat the baked chiffon sponge layers using the vanilla meringue buttercream, as per the instructions on page 172. Chill for 30 minutes or until set.

Once the crumb coat has set, mask the cake with a perfectly smooth and even layer of buttercream. This time, apply a slightly thicker coat of buttercream around the sides. (Reserve a little buttercream for sticking the nests to the cake.) Go around a few times if not perfect the first time. Transfer the cake back to the fridge and chill until the buttercream has set.

Mix the cocoa powder with the hot water to a thick brown liquid. Dip a flat artist's brush inside, hold the brush near the cake and flick the bristles into the direction of the cake until it is covered with brown speckles.

Arrange 10 evenly-spaced chocolate nests around the top of the cake, sticking them down with dabs of buttercream.

SPRING & EASTER STYLE SECRETS

There is such natural beauty at this time of year, and you really just need to spend some time wandering pretty neighbourhood streets, or strolling through local parks to find all the inspiration you need. In Germany, creating an Easter Tree at home has been a long-held tradition and it's a beautiful way of marking the arrival of spring. Simply find a collection of branches from a garden or park and arrange them at home in a tall vase. You can even spray your branches white or pastel depending on your theme. In Germany, an Easter Tree is called an 'Osterbaum' and it's decorated with beautifully coloured eggs. There are lots of ways to get creative here, from purchasing pastel eggs that will be used year after year, to having fun with the children hand-painting white egg ornaments with your own designs. You can even find small bird nest decorations from floristry suppliers and they make for an adorable addition to your tree. If you're feeling extra creative, why not paint a birdhouse in pastel colours and decorate it with faux garden birds and coloured eggs?

♡

Over the years, I have gathered an impressive collection of white ceramic bunnies in various shapes and sizes. I find they are timeless and fit into any style and theme we choose for Easter. As I've mentioned before, I love to tell little stories through our Parlour collections and installations, which is an idea that can easily be replicated at home. I am always drawn to the playful yet comforting stories of Beatrix Potter during spring, and using small decorative garden animals amongst your arrangement is a wonderful way to bring this to life for children. I'm hugely passionate about nature, and I love the discussions that can be drawn out as to why our wildlife and ecosystems must be cherished. Another 'collector's item' for me, which comes in very handy at Easter, is my selection of wicker baskets. I often spray them in white or pastel colours to match my colour scheme. They make a beautiful gift when filled with a collection of adorable Chirpy Chick Cookies (see page 30).

Vegan Jam Heart Cookies

Elevating a childhood favourite, these yummy cookies are easy to make and have a satisfying crunch, making them a perfect teatime treat. For anyone using plant-based margarine for the first time, it's worth noting that it makes a softer textured dough and can melt quickly at room temperature. It's therefore important to work quickly and not stretch your cut-out cookie shapes. For a non-vegan version, the margarine can be replaced with butter. These cookies make a very sweet gift and keep well in an airtight container for up to three weeks.

MAKES 15 COOKIES

200g (7oz/¾ cup plus 2 tbsp) sunflower margarine, cold
300g (10½oz/2¼ cups) plain (all-purpose) flour, sifted, plus extra for dusting
100g (3½oz/½ cup) caster sugar
pinch of salt
1 tsp vanilla extract
75g (2½oz/5 tbsp) redcurrant or raspberry jelly

Specialist equipment (see page 164 for a basic equipment list and page 182 for stockists)
round pastry cutter, about 6cm (2½in) diameter
small heart-shaped cutter, about 2.5cm (1in) diameter

TO MAKE THE COOKIES

Dice the cold margarine and place it in a large bowl. Mix the flour with the sugar and salt and sprinkle it over the cold margarine.

Rub the flour mix into the margarine with your fingertips until the texture looks evenly crumbly. Add the vanilla extract and knead the mixture to a dough.

Wrap the dough in cling film, flatten it and chill for at least 1 hour, or until the dough feels cold and firm.

Meanwhile, preheat the oven to 175°C fan/375°F/ Gas 5 and line 2 baking trays with baking parchment.

Lightly dust a smooth cool work surface with flour and roll the dough out to a thickness of about 3mm (⅛in).

Using the round cookie cutter, stamp out about 30 rounds and place them onto the prepared baking trays.

Using the small heart shaped cutter, stamp a heart centre out of half of the cookies.

Chill the cookies again for 15 minutes until cool and set.

Bake in the preheated oven for 6–8 minutes until golden brown. Turn your trays halfway through baking to ensure an even colouration. Once cooked, allow to cool completely on the trays.

TO FILL THE COOKIES

Heat the jelly in a small saucepan or in the microwave – it should be smooth and hot. Spread 1 tsp of the jelly into the middle of each whole round cookie using a teaspoon. Place a cookie with a heart cutout on top while the jelly is still hot and allow it to set.

Ring O' Roses
PINK PROSECCO CAKE

I designed this elegant cake for Mother's Day a few years ago and ever since it has become a Peggy Porschen favourite when celebrating special occasions. Pastel pink rose-flavoured buttercream is bevelled around the sides and topped with a ring of pretty wafer roses. The inner cake reveals light and fluffy chiffon sponge infused with prosecco syrup and layered with rose meringue buttercream. The timeless quality of this cake makes it a recipe to keep coming back to.

MAKES A 15CM (6IN) CAKE (SERVES 10)

1 quantity Chiffon Sponge (3 x 15cm/6in cakes, see page 171) flavoured with 1 tsp vanilla extract

For the rosé prosecco sugar syrup

100g (3½oz/½ cup) caster sugar
50ml (1¾fl oz/3½ tbsp) water
50ml (1¾fl oz/3½ tbsp) rosé prosecco

For the rose meringue buttercream

1 layer cake quantity Meringue Buttercream (see page 176)
rosewater, to taste
pink food colouring paste

For the decorations

10 pink wafer rose buds (see Stockists, page 182)
10 green wafer leaves (see Stockists, page 182)
pearl edible lustre spray (see Stockists, page 182)

Specialist equipment (see page 164 for a basic equipment list and page 182 for stockists)

3 x 15cm (6in) shallow cake tins
15cm (6in) thin cake board
bevelled buttercream comb
large piping bag fitted with a small star nozzle

TO MAKE THE ROSÉ PROSECCO SUGAR SYRUP

Put the sugar and water in a saucepan, bring to a boil and cook until the sugar is dissolved. Remove from the heat and allow to cool.

Once cool, add the rosé prosecco.

TO MAKE THE ROSE MERINGUE BUTTERCREAM

Add a few drops of rosewater to the meringue buttercream, to taste.

Mix 1 tbsp of the buttercream with a small amount of pink food colouring to achieve a bright pink shade and blend together with a palette knife until all the colour specks have dispersed.

Little by little, add the pink buttercream back to the main batch and mix until you have reached a pretty pastel pink.

TO ASSEMBLE AND DECORATE THE CAKE

Layer and crumb coat the baked chiffon sponge layers using the rose meringue buttercream and the rosé prosecco sugar syrup, as per the instructions on page 172. Chill for 30 minutes or until set.

Once the crumb coat has set, mask the cake with a perfectly smooth and even layer of buttercream. This time, apply a slightly thicker coat of buttercream around the sides and use a bevelled buttercream comb to scrape around it. Go around a few times if not perfect the first time. Transfer the cake back to the fridge and chill until the buttercream has set.

Spoon the remaining buttercream into a piping bag fitted with a small star nozzle.

Pipe 10 evenly-sized and -spaced out rosettes of buttercream around the top of the cake and decorate each with a rose bud and leaf.

Sweet Summer

Summer really is a mood lifter at the Parlours. It's always the most eagerly anticipated time of year for us due to the vibrant colours, fabulous florals bursting into bloom and summertime fruits found throughout our locations. With many Londoners not having access to their own gardens, we are able to offer this connection to nature as a seasonal feast for all the senses.

I am always spoilt for choice with flavours at this time of year. To guide my recipe selection, I have introduced some of the Parlours' most popular bakes, whilst ensuring that there are variations for different levels of baking. Choose the Summer Berry Cupcake for its beautiful burst of berry flavour and vibrant colour, or select the Cherry & Chocolate Drip Cake for an impressive bake that is as decadent as it is moreish. I adore using elderflower and have included our Lemon Elderflower Tartlet. I have always loved a good lemon tart, and this one was created in honour of the wedding of Prince Harry and Meghan Markle. And for those looking for a show-stopping recipe, the Berries & 'Elderfleur' Cake is, for me, the ultimate in summertime beauty, elegance and taste.

We often describe the Parlours as 'a world where roses always bloom' and I always feel that summertime is when this really comes to life. Our floral installations and cakes unite in such synchronisation that it creates a dream-like air of awe and wonder. I truly hope that this infectious happiness is felt in the baking and sharing of the recipes found in this chapter.

Floral Hoop Cookies

This recipe is all about flower power. The flavours of lemon, lavender and honey make for a delectable cookie base whilst the royal icing and edible flower top is a simple technique with impressive results. Dried edible flowers and petals are now widely available in shops and online, however if you are lucky enough to have them growing in your garden, you can also dry your own by pressing them in between the pages of a heavy book.

MAKES 12 COOKIES

For the honey, lemon and lavender shortbread

155g (5½oz/⅔ cup) unsalted butter, diced
1 tsp salt
80g (2¾oz/¼ cup) honey
50g (1¾oz/¼ cup) caster sugar
225g (8oz/1¾ cups) plain (all-purpose) flour, sifted, plus extra for dusting
25g (1oz) lemon zest, finely grated (about 3 lemons)
25ml (1fl oz/1 tbsp plus 2 tsp) lemon juice (about ½ squeezed lemon)
1 tsp dried culinary lavender

For the lemon icing

300g (10½oz) Royal Icing (see page 167)
1 tsp lemon juice
magenta food colouring paste (see Stockists, page 182)

For the decoration

dehydrated edible petals, such as yellow calendula, blue cornflower, pink carnation, orange marigold (see Stockists, page 182)
12 dried cornflower blossoms or carnations (you can also dry your own flowers from the garden)
2 tbsp freeze-dried raspberries, crushed
50g (1¾oz/½ cup) chopped pistachios

Specialist equipment (see page 164 for a basic equipment list and page 182 for stockists)

10cm (4in) and 4cm (1½in) round fluted cookie cutters
2 piping bags, or make 2 of your own paper piping bags (see page 168)

TO MAKE THE COOKIES

Put the butter, salt, honey and sugar in the bowl of an electric mixer fitted with a paddle attachment and cream together until pale.

Add the flour and gently mix until just combined, then add the lemon zest and juice and the lavender. Mix briefly to incorporate.

Bring the mixture together to form a dough, wrap it in cling film and chill for at least 30 minutes.

Preheat the oven to 175°C fan/375°F/Gas 5 and line 2 baking trays with baking parchment.

Place the cookie dough on a lightly-floured work surface and roll it out to an even thickness of about 5mm (¼in).

Using the 2 sizes of cookie cutters, stamp out 12 cookie hoops and place them onto the lined baking trays, spaced apart by at least 1cm (½in). Ensure that there are no wrinkles in the paper under the cookies and weigh the edges of the paper down if using a fan-assisted oven, otherwise the cookies may lift up during the baking process and turn out uneven. Put the trays of cookies in the fridge to chill for about 10 minutes.

Bake in the preheated oven for 8–12 minutes, turning the trays once during baking to ensure they bake evenly. When cooked, they should look golden brown and spring back when pressing down with your finger. Allow the cookies to cool on the trays.

TO DECORATE THE COOKIES

Mix the royal icing with a small amount of the magenta pink food colouring to a soft pink shade.

Mix 1 tbsp of the pink icing with a small amount of water to a soft peak piping consistency (see page 167 for a guide to royal icing consistencies). Spoon it into a piping bag and snip a small tip off the end. Pipe an outline around the inner and outer edges of each cookie.

Dilute the remaining pink icing with a few drops of lemon juice to achieve a runny flooding consistency. Spoon it into another piping bag. Snip a small tip off the piping bag and use it to flood the area between the piped outlines with the runny icing. As you are squeezing the icing inside the outline, watch it flow slowly across the cookie and ensure that you don't overfill as the runny icing might spill over the edges.

While the icing is still wet, sprinkle the edible petals and flowers on top, followed by a sprinkle of crushed raspberries and chopped pistachios.

Let the icing dry, ideally overnight. Store in a dry place at room temperature.

TIP

If you are not a very experienced piper, simply dilute all of the royal icing with the lemon juice to a runny consistency and carefully dip the top of the cookies in. When lifting a cookie out, drizzle off the excess by spinning the cookie in your hand. Swiftly flip over, place on a wire rack and sprinkle with the edible petals, raspberries and pistachios, then leave to set until the icing is dry.

If you're dipping the cookies in icing in this way, you can achieve a marbled effect by not completely mixing the pink colouring into the royal icing (you will need a little more than stated in the recipe to have enough depth of icing for dipping).

Lemon & Yogurt Loaves

These little loaf cakes taste like summer on a plate and are the perfect project for novice bakers. The sponge is made with fresh lemon zest and Greek-style yogurt, making it light, lemony and moist. The pastel lemon icing adds extra zing and the dried edible petals add a striking finishing touch. Thank you to Harriet Webster for modelling in the photograph opposite!

MAKES 12 MINI LOAF CAKES

For the loaf cakes
210g (7½oz/1 cup plus 1 tbsp) caster sugar
105g (3½oz/7 tbsp) unsalted butter, softened, plus extra for greasing
finely grated zest and freshly squeezed juice of 1½ unwaxed lemons
2 large eggs, at room temperature
150g (5⅓oz/1 cup) plain (all-purpose) flour, sifted, plus extra for dusting
¼ tsp salt
¼ tsp bicarbonate of soda (baking soda)
¼ tsp baking powder
115g (4oz/½ cup less 1 tbsp) Greek-style yogurt

For the sugar glaze
2 tbsp smooth apricot jam
150g (5⅓oz/1 cup plus 1 tbsp) icing (confectioner's) sugar, sifted
freshly squeezed juice of ½ lemon
pink food colouring paste (optional)
1 tsp dried culinary lavender
1 tbsp dried edible flower petals (such as dianthus, viola and cornflower)

Specialist equipment (see page 164 for a basic equipment list and page 182 for stockists)
12 x mini loaf baking tins (about 8 x 4 x 4cm/ 3¼ x 1½ x 1½in)

TO MAKE THE LOAF CAKES

Preheat the oven to 175°C fan/375°F/Gas 5. Grease the tins with butter, then dust with flour.

Put the sugar, butter and lemon zest into a bowl and cream together until pale and fluffy. Beat the eggs, then gradually add them to the butter mixture, making sure they are fully incorporated.

Combine the flour, salt, bicarbonate of soda and baking powder and add to the mixture in 3 batches, mixing well between each addition.

Add the lemon juice and yogurt to the batter and mix well. Divide the batter evenly between the loaf tins, filling each one about three-quarters full.

Bake in the preheated oven for 15–20 minutes, until the tops are golden and spring back to the touch. Rest for about 15 minutes in the tins, then unmould and leave to cool completely on a wire rack.

TO MAKE THE SUGAR GLAZE

Heat the apricot jam in the microwave or in a small saucepan until very hot and smooth. Brush the top of each loaf cake with a thin layer of the jam and leave to set.

Mix the icing sugar with enough of the lemon juice to make a thick, runny glaze.

Mix a small amount of pink food colouring into the icing to make a pretty pink shade. Be careful not to add too much colouring – paste colour is more concentrated than liquid colour.

Spoon or pour the coloured icing on top of the cakes and allow it to drip down the sides. Sprinkle with the lavender and edible flower petals while the icing is still wet.

Queen Bee

CHOCOLATE & HONEY CUPCAKES

Chocolate and honey is a sumptuous combination. This recipe unites a rich, smooth chocolate sponge with a sweet honey filling and a smooth 'beehive' swirl of cream cheese and honey frosting. Pretty golden honeybees and sugar blossoms add a playful touch and make these cupcakes the perfect treat for any queen bee in your life.

MAKES 24 CUPCAKES

For the decorations

150g (5½oz) white sugar florist paste
a small amount of white vegetable fat (eg Trex)
icing (confectioner's) sugar and cornflour (cornstarch),
  for dusting
1 tbsp Royal Icing (see page 167)
yellow food colouring paste
gold edible lustre powder (see Stockists, page 182)
2 tbsp popping candy (see Stockists, page 182)
gold edible lustre spray (see Stockists, page 182)

For the chocolate cupcakes

105g (3½oz/7 tbsp) unsalted butter, softened
285g (10oz/1½ cups less 1 tbsp) light brown sugar
125g (4½oz) dark chocolate (53% cocoa solids),
  chopped or in buttons
165ml (5¼fl oz/⅔ cup) whole milk
2 large eggs
180g (6¼oz/1⅓ cups) plain (all-purpose) flour
½ tsp baking powder
½ tsp bicarbonate of soda (baking soda)
pinch of salt
1 tbsp cocoa powder

For the honey meringue buttercream

1 cupcake quantity Meringue Buttercream
  (see page 176)
100g (3½oz/6 tbsp) honey

For the filling

250g (9oz/¾ cup) honey

**Specialist equipment (see page 164 for a basic
  equipment list and page 182 for stockists)**

small 5-petal blossom cutter
flower foam pad
balling tool
piping bag, or make your own paper piping bag
  (see page 168)
bee silicone mould
24 brown paper baking cases
2 x 12-hole cupcake baking trays
large piping bag fitted with a large round nozzle

TO MAKE THE DECORATIONS

Take the sugar florist paste out of the packet and check for any dry and crumbly bits of paste. Trim them off with a knife to ensure they don't get mixed into the paste as they will spoil the whole batch.

Rub a small amount of white vegetable fat between your hands before kneading the sugar florist paste until smooth. Should the paste stick, add a little more vegetable fat. Wrap in cling film and rest for about 10 minutes to allow it to firm up slightly.

To make the sugar blossoms, lightly rub a smooth surface or plastic board with cornflour and place the sugar florist paste on top. Apply a thin layer of vegetable fat to a small rolling pin and roll the paste out to a thickness of 1mm (1/32in).

Using the 5-petal blossom cutter, stamp out 2 blossoms per cupcake, about 50 altogether. As the paste will dry quickly, stamp out a few blossoms at a time and keep the remaining paste covered.

Place the blossoms onto the flower foam pad and thin the individual petals with the balling tool. Ensure you keep the petal sizes even and avoid over stretching.

Lightly dust the wells of a colour mixing palette with icing sugar or cornflour and place one blossom into each well to let them set in a cup shape.

Mix the royal icing with a tiny amount of yellow food colouring paste to a light yellow. Add a drop of water and mix the icing to a soft peak consistency using a small palette knife (for guidance on royal icing consistencies, see page 167).

Spoon the royal icing into a piping bag, snip a small tip off the end and pipe a small yellow dot of icing into the centre of each sugar blossom. Leave them to dry.

To make the sugar bees, mix the remaining florist paste with a small amount of yellow food colouring paste to a creamy light shade of yellow.

Rub the inner part of the bee silicone mould with a thin layer of vegetable fat. Pinch a small amount off the paste, roll it into a smooth ball and press it into the bee mould. Flatten the back of the bee and trim off any excess. To release the bee, bend the mould outward until it drops out.

While still soft, brush the bee with edible gold lustre powder using a soft artist's brush and leave to dry. Make 24 sugar bees altogether.

To make the gold nuggets, tip the popping candy into a small bowl and sprinkle with gold lustre powder. Use a big soft artist's brush to evenly coat them in gold lustre until completely covered.

TO MAKE THE CHOCOLATE CUPCAKES

Preheat the oven to 160°C fan/350°F/Gas 4 and line the cupcake trays with the baking cases.

Put the butter and half of the sugar into the bowl of an electric mixer fitted with a paddle attachment and cream together until pale and fluffy. This will take a while, so do this as a first step to allow plenty of time to aerate the mixture.

Put the chocolate, milk and the remaining sugar into a small saucepan and bring to a light simmer, stirring occasionally to ensure the chocolate doesn't burn.

Beat the eggs in a separate bowl, and slowly add to the butter and sugar mixture.

Sift together the flour, baking powder, bicarbonate of soda, salt and cocoa powder. Add this to the butter and sugar mixture in 2 batches, still mixing at low speed and waiting until the first batch is combined before adding the next.

Once the chocolate has melted and the mixture has come to a light simmer, remove the pan from the heat and slowly pour the chocolate milk into the batter while still mixing at low speed. Be careful not to splash yourself with any hot liquid. Scrape the bottom of the mixing bowl with a rubber spatula to ensure that everything is well combined.

Transfer the chocolate batter into a large jug and pour the mix into the baking cases, filling each one two-thirds full.

Transfer the trays to the preheated oven immediately while the batter is still warm and bake for 15–20 minutes, depending on your oven. The cupcakes are cooked when the tops spring back to the touch and the edges of the baking cases have shrunk away from the sides of the baking tray. The texture should be soft and slightly sticky, so if inserting a knife to test if cooked, there should be a small amount of crumb sticking to the blade.

Remove from the oven and leave to rest in the cupcake trays for a few minutes.

Transfer the cupcakes to a wire rack and leave to cool completely.

When cool, chill for 30 minutes to firm the sponge up a little.

TO MAKE THE HONEY MERINGUE BUTTERCREAM

Add the honey to the meringue buttercream and whisk until well combined.

TO FILL AND DECORATE THE CUPCAKES

Scoop a small well out of the centre of each cupcake using a melon baller.

Fill each cupcake with 1 tsp of honey.

Spoon the honey meringue buttercream into a large piping bag fitted with a large round nozzle. Pipe a generous beehive-shaped swirl on top of each cupcake.

Spray one side of each buttercream beehive with the edible gold lustre spray for a gradual golden colouration.

Place 2 sugar blossoms, one bee and a sprinkle of gold nuggets on top of each beehive.

Serve as soon as possible or chill for about 30 minutes until the buttercream has slightly set before transporting them. Always serve and enjoy at room temperature. The sugar bees and blossoms may melt if exposed to humidity and should be consumed within 24 hours once placed on a cupcake.

TIP

It's important to bake the cupcakes as soon as possible after transferring the warm batter to the baking cases, otherwise the baked cupcakes are likely to develop dry crusts on top. If this does happen, brush the tops of the cupcakes with a light sugar syrup after baking to soften them.

Summer Berry Cupcakes

Our summer berry cupcake has become a firm favourite at the Parlour over the past few years. It's no surprise as it's bursting with juicy berry flavours and decorated with vibrant pinks and purples. The buttermilk sponge ensures a light and gentle texture making this a go-to recipe for anyone wanting to have fun with classic summer tastes.

MAKES 24 CUPCAKES

For the vanilla sugar syrup

150g (5½oz/¾ cup) caster sugar
150ml (5fl oz/scant ⅔ cup) water
1 tsp vanilla extract

For the summer berry buttermilk cupcakes

1 cupcake quantity Buttermilk Sponge batter (see page 170) – follow the instructions up to the stage when you've finished the batter
about 2 punnets of fresh raspberries
about 1 punnet of fresh blueberries

For the summer berry meringue buttercream

30g (1oz) Raspberry Purée (see page 179) made with 60g (2oz) raspberries, cooled
30g (1oz) Strawberry Purée (see page 179) made with 60g (2oz) strawberries, cooled
30g (1oz) Blueberry Purée (see page 179) made with 40g (1½oz) blueberries, cooled

1 cupcake quantity Meringue Buttercream (see page 176)

For the decoration

2 tbsp freeze-dried raspberries, crushed
12 medium-sized fresh strawberries
24 fresh raspberries
24 fresh blueberries
24 edible carnation flowers (or you can use any other edible fresh flower decorations, such as violets or pansies)

Specialist equipment (see page 164 for a basic equipment list and page 182 for stockists)

2 x 12-hole cupcake trays
24 red paper baking cases
large piping bag
large piping bag fitted with a large star nozzle

TO MAKE THE VANILLA SUGAR SYRUP

Put the sugar, water and vanilla extract in a saucepan, bring to a boil and cook until the sugar is dissolved. Remove from the heat and allow to cool.

TO BAKE THE SUMMER BERRY BUTTERMILK CUPCAKES

Preheat the oven to 175°C fan/375°F/Gas 5 and line the cupcake trays with baking cases.

Fill a large piping bag with the batter and snip 2.5cm (1in) off the tip. Pipe the batter into the baking cases, filling each one about two-thirds full.

Drop 1–2 large raspberries and 2–3 blueberries on top of each cupcake.

Bake in the preheated oven for about 15 minutes, depending on your oven. The cupcakes are cooked when they are golden, the tops spring back to the touch and the edges of the baking cases have shrunk away from the sides of the baking tray.

Remove from the oven and leave to rest in the cupcake trays for a few minutes.

Brush the tops of the cakes with the vanilla sugar syrup while still hot. This will ensure the sponges absorb the moisture and prevent a dry crust from forming.

Transfer the cupcakes to a wire rack and leave to cool completely. Wipe the bottoms with a damp cloth if sticky from the syrup. Do not leave the cupcakes to cool in the cupcake tray, as the cases may stick to the tray.

TO MAKE THE SUMMER BERRY MERINGUE BUTTERCREAM

Mix the cooled berry purées together and carefully mix into the meringue buttercream. Ensure that the purée and buttercream are at the same room temperature to prevent the mixture from splitting.

TO DECORATE THE CUPCAKES

Spoon the summer berry meringue buttercream into a large piping bag with a large star nozzle and pipe a rosette on top of each cupcake.

Sprinkle the crushed freeze-dried raspberries over the top.

Cut the strawberries in half and place half a strawberry on top of each rosette, followed by a raspberry and blueberry. Add an edible flower to each cupcake.

Serve as soon as possible or chill for about 30 minutes until the buttercream has slightly set before transporting them. Always serve and enjoy at room temperature. Store in the fridge if not eaten right away and consume within 24 hours.

TIP

To prevent the strawberries from drying out, brush the cut surface with apricot jam.

CREATE A NEST

Writing this whilst still living with the challenges of the Covid pandemic,
I've become even more aware of how important personal space is. I, like all those
living with family, have been desperate at times for a small space of my own where
I can relax, unwind and be creative. Equally for those living alone, this clear space
to feel cocooned and tranquil is a precious thing. I like to think of this as a 'hush corner'
or a nest. It could be a small room, if you're lucky enough to have this space, and if
not, it could even be a small nook, next to a window. Somewhere where you can
keep a comfortable chair and a spot for your coffee, book, notepad or whatever it
is that lets you unwind and switch off.

Even if you don't have a private garden – which we don't, like so many living in
London – I do find that the ability to sit either on a balcony, or next to an open
window to feel the breeze and observe the season brings a sense of calm. Since
it has become a frequent trend for shop and restaurant fronts to install floral arches,
I have noticed lots of homes around the area that I live in in London, near Battersea
Park, creating little floral features on their balconies or around entrance doors. This
connection to nature is so important in giving a sense of reassurance and peace.

Cherry Choc Chip Cupcakes

With a satisfying 'cherry on top', this cupcake is all frills. Here, chocolate chip sponge is filled with cherry jam and iced with a tutu-esque cherry frosting using a Russian ball tip piping nozzle. It practically pirouettes off the plate at you!

MAKES 24 CUPCAKES

For the vanilla sugar syrup
150g (5½oz/¾ cup) caster sugar
150ml (5fl oz/scant ⅔ cup) water
1 tsp vanilla extract

For the chocolate chip cupcakes
225g (8oz/1 cup) unsalted butter, softened
225g (8oz/1 cup plus 2 tbsp) caster sugar
pinch of salt
1 tsp vanilla extract
4 medium eggs, at room temperature
225g (8oz/1¾ cups) self-raising flour, sifted
80g (2¾oz) dark chocolate chips (53% cocoa solids), roughly chopped

For the filling
240g (8½oz) good-quality cherry jam

For the cherry meringue buttercream
125g (4½oz) Cherry Purée (see page 179), made from 400g (14oz) pitted fresh or frozen cherries, cooled
1 cupcake quantity Meringue Buttercream (see page 176)

For the decoration
24 fresh cherries with stalks
about 100g (3½oz) dark chocolate shavings (or shave your own from a chocolate bar using a peeler)

Specialist equipment (see page 164 for a basic equipment list and page 182 for stockists)
2 x 12-hole cupcake baking trays
24 metallic pink baking cases
large piping bag
large piping bag fitted with a small star nozzle
large piping bag fitted with a Russian ball tip piping nozzle

TO MAKE THE SUGAR SYRUP

Put the sugar, water and vanilla extract in a saucepan, bring to a boil and cook until the sugar is dissolved. Remove from the heat and allow to cool.

TO MAKE THE CHOCOLATE CHIP CUPCAKES

Preheat the oven to 175°C fan/375°F/Gas 5 and line the cupcake trays with the baking cases.

Put the butter, sugar, salt and vanilla extract in the bowl of an electric mixer fitted with a paddle attachment and cream together until pale and fluffy.

Beat the eggs in a separate bowl, and slowly add to the butter and sugar mixture, making sure they are fully incorporated before adding more, and the mixture doesn't split.

Fold the flour into the batter in 3 additions, then add the chocolate chips.

Fill a large piping bag with the batter and snip 2.5cm (1in) off the tip. Pipe the batter into the baking cases, filling each one about two-thirds full. Start in the centre of the base of the case, then move the piping bag up and around the outside of the case, leaving a dip in the middle; this will ensure that the cupcakes rise more evenly.

Tap the tray down a couple of times on the work surface and leave to rest for 10 minutes before baking them (I find that this prevents the cupcakes from rising too high and cracking open at the top during the baking process).

Bake in the preheated oven for 12–15 minutes. The cupcakes are cooked when they are golden, the tops spring back to the touch and the edges of the baking cases have shrunk away from the sides of the baking tray.

Remove from the oven and leave to rest for a few minutes in the trays.

Brush the tops of the cakes with the vanilla syrup while still hot. This will ensure the sponges absorb the moisture and prevent a dry crust from forming.

Transfer the cupcakes onto a wire rack and leave to cool completely. Wipe the bottoms with a damp cloth if sticky from the syrup.

Chill in the fridge for about 30 minutes to slightly firm up the sponge.

Scoop a small well out of the centre of each cupcake using a melon baller.

Fill the cupcake centres with 1 tsp cherry jam each.

TIP

Do not let the cupcakes cool completely inside the baking tray as the paper will stick to the bottom and tear when unmoulding.

TO MAKE THE CHERRY MERINGUE BUTTERCREAM

Transfer about 2 heaped tbsp of the meringue buttercream from the main batch into a piping bag fitted with the star nozzle and set aside – this will be used for the rosettes.

Slowly add the cherry purée to the remaining buttercream and mix until well combined. Ensure that the purée and buttercream are at the same room temperature to prevent the mixture from splitting.

TO DECORATE THE CUPCAKES

Spoon the cherry buttercream into a piping bag fitted with the Russian ball tip piping nozzle. Hold the piping bag vertically above the centre of a cupcake and squeeze the bag firmly but slowly, so that the buttercream squeezes out with some pressure that will help create a voluminous ruffled rosette. Once the rosette has spread in width to cover about two-thirds of the cupcake top, gradually lift the bag as you continue to squeeze out the ruffles. As you reach the desired height, release the pressure and pull the bag up. Repeat to cover all of the cupcakes.

Take the piping bag fitted with the star nozzle and filled with the plain buttercream and pipe a small rosette on top of the pink ruffles on each cupcake.

Decorate the top of each cupcake with a fresh cherry, then sprinkle with the chocolate shavings.

Serve as soon as possible or chill for about 30 minutes until the buttercream has slightly set before transporting them. Always serve and enjoy at room temperature. Store in the fridge if not eaten right away and consume within 24 hours.

Lemon Elderflower Tartlets

I love a good lemon tart and it would always be my number one choice from any dessert menu. So when Prince Harry and Meghan Markle got married back in 2018, I came up with a lemon and elderflower version inspired by the flavours of the royal wedding cake. Topped with lemon meringue kisses and fresh elderflowers, my tartlet has been given extra special 'Markle sparkle' treatment with a sprinkling of golden popping candy.

MAKES 12 TARTLETS

For the lemon meringue kisses

1 quantity Meringue Kisses (see page 180) – follow the instructions up to the stage at which you're ready to add the flavouring
lemon extract (see Stockists, page 182), to taste
yellow food colouring paste

For the tartlet shells

150g (5½oz/⅔ cup) unsalted butter, softened, plus extra for greasing
300g (10½oz/2¼ cups) plain (all-purpose) flour, sifted, plus extra for dusting and flouring the tins
120g (4¼oz/¾ cup plus 2 tbsp) icing (confectioner's) sugar, sifted
2 medium eggs, at room temperature
½ tsp vanilla extract
pinch of salt

For the lemon and elderflower custard

245ml (8fl oz/1 cup) freshly squeezed lemon juice and grated zest, from approx. 5 lemons, strained

3 medium eggs
245g (9oz/1¼ cups) caster sugar
25g (1oz/2 tbsp) custard powder
100g (3½oz/½ cup less 1 tbsp) unsalted butter, softened
20 drops of elderflower extract (see Stockists, page 182)

For the decoration

icing (confectioner's) sugar, for dusting
fresh edible elderflower blossoms
2 tbsp popping candy
edible gold lustre dust
silver metallic sugar balls (4mm/⅛in)

Specialist equipment (see page 164 for a basic equipment list and page 182 for stockists)

large piping bag fitted with a small open star nozzle
large piping bag fitted with a large narrow star nozzle
large piping bag fitted with a large round nozzle
12 x 10cm (4in) round tartlet tins
interlocking circles stencil

TO MAKE THE LEMON MERINGUE KISSES

Preheat the oven to 80°C/175°F/Gas ¼.

Add a drop of lemon extract to the meringue mix.

Spoon one-third of the meringue from the batch into a piping bag fitted with a small open star nozzle – this will stay white.

Mix about 1 tbsp of the remaining meringue with a drop of yellow food colour and blend together with a palette knife until all the colour specks have dispersed. Add this back into the meringue and mix in until you have an even pale yellow shade.

Spoon half of the yellow meringue into a piping bag fitted with a large narrow star nozzle. Spoon the other yellow half into a piping bag fitted with a large round nozzle.

Pipe the white meringue into small star meringue kisses on a prepared baking tray. Pipe the yellow meringue with the large round nozzle into small yellow round kisses on another baking tray – the bases should be about 1.5cm (just over ½in). Use the piping bag with the large narrow star to pipe larger kisses – the bases should be just under 2cm (¾in). The difference in size can be achieved by squeezing the bag for longer to increase the size.

Bake for about 1 hour, or until the meringues can be lifted clean off the tray. Allow to cool.

TO MAKE THE TARTLET SHELLS

Grease the tartlet tins with butter and lightly dust with flour. Chill the tins while you make the pastry.

Put the butter and icing sugar in the bowl of an electric mixer fitted with a paddle attachment and cream together until combined.

Add the eggs, one at a time, followed by the vanilla extract.

Slowly add the flour and salt.

When the mix has come together, transfer the dough to a smooth, lightly floured work surface. Shape it into a ball and work it with your hands, stretching it and regathering it for a short while. This will work the gluten in the flour and toughen the dough slightly, which will make the tartlet shells crisper after baking. Wrap the dough in cling film and chill for 30 minutes.

Divide the dough into 10 even pieces and, one at a time, roll each out with a rolling pin on a surface lightly dusted with flour to a thickness of about 3–4mm (⅛in). Lay the pastry over the tartlet tins and gently push down the middle and sides using a small piece of dough. Trim the excess off using a kitchen knife. Prick the bases with a fork and chill for 20 minutes. Preheat the oven to 175°C fan/375°F/ Gas 5.

Bake the pastry cases in the preheated oven for 10–12 minutes, or until golden brown. Leave the pastry cases to cool on a wire rack, then unmould from the tins when completely cool.

TO MAKE THE LEMON AND ELDERFLOWER CUSTARD

Put the lemon juice and zest in a saucepan and bring to a boil.

Put the eggs and two-thirds of the sugar into a heatproof bowl and whisk together.

In a separate bowl, mix the remaining sugar with the custard powder. Add the sugar and custard powder mix to the eggs and whisk until combined.

Pour the boiling lemon juice into the egg mix, whisking continuously until combined.

Pour everything back into the saucepan and slowly bring it back to the boil. Cook for about 5 minutes while whisking constantly.

When the custard has thickened, remove the pan from the heat and transfer the custard to a bowl. Place a sugar thermometer in the custard and cover as much of the top of the custard as possible with cling film to prevent a skin forming. Let it cool down to 59°C/138°F.

Once cooled, add the soft butter, a little at a time, while blending the custard with a stick blender to emulsify the mixture.

Add a few drops of elderflower extract to taste.

Use the lemon custard to fill the tartlet shells and level the tops off with a palette knife. Place in the fridge to cool.

TO DECORATE THE TARTLETS

Decorate your tartlets shortly before serving them. Place the stencil loosely on top of a tartlet and dust the gaps with icing sugar. Repeat for all of them.

Place the popping candy in a bowl and sprinkle with gold lustre powder. Use a big, soft artist's brush to coat the popping candy evenly. Scatter over the tartlets. Finally, decorate each tartlet with one of each of the meringue kisses, a small sprig of fresh edible elderflowers and silver metallic balls.

STENCIL ART

Another easy but effective styling ritual that we follow at the Parlours is to use coffee stencils to decorate appropriate drinks such as cappuccinos. We always custom-create stencils to match our latest seasonal theme, and it gives a well-rounded look to our photography, but most importantly, it gives an extra dose of happiness to our customers.

At home, this is easy, too. You can buy off-the-shelf stencils in all sorts of shapes, for example, hearts for Valentine's, an egg for Easter, and a leaf for autumn. What's more, stencils are not only handy for 'dressing up' coffees, they are also a simple way of decorating tartlets, cookies and cake tops.
I've included some of my favourite suppliers at the end of the book.

SUMMER STYLING TIPS

British summertime, for me, is all about eating al fresco as much as possible. From picnics in the park to garden parties at home, this is the time to really enjoy the outdoors, collecting happy memories of warm days and long evenings. I can never say 'no' to a pretty picnic blanket and a wicker basket overflowing with seasonal tastes. This is an easy way to entertain at home, or in the park, and sets the scene for an elevated picnic experience. Make lots of iced tea and summery cream tea treats, such as simple but lovingly prepared finger sandwiches and scones. My miniature Lemon & Yogurt Loaves (see page 60) make the perfect 'outdoors pudding' as they come in individual portions and are picture perfect with their petal confetti tops.

♡

If the weather holds and you have a balcony or small garden, bunting and fairy lights will take you well into the evening. I adore a shabby chic bistro table and chair set to add to the romantic tone. You could even create a mini flower meadow with lots of potted plants; the honey bees will love it, and it's very grounding to watch them busily filling their little pollen baskets. My key investments for summer would also be a straw hat, a pretty tea dress and a pink bicycle, with a large wicker basket. I love bicycles by English manufacturer Pashley Cycles, and this is the one that has featured in our summer Parlour displays. These accessories will complete the picture when you pop in and out of local stores, picking up beautiful fresh flowers and ingredients for your summertime bakes. It's also a look that is as practical as it is pretty, for stretching out on a picnic blanket and soaking up the dreamy summertime atmosphere.

Blueberry Custard Tartlets

This is an elegant chocolate tartlet filled with creamy blueberry custard and garnished with fresh blueberries, summer meringue kisses and edible violets. What I love about this chic tartlet are the deep colours of dark brown and purple set off against the pastel pink meringue kisses. Violet pansies make an exquisite colour match as decorations, but any edible summer garden blossom or petals will also look very pretty.

MAKES 12 TARTLETS

For the blueberry meringue kisses

1 quantity Meringue Kisses (see page 180) – follow the instructions up to the stage at which you're ready to add the flavouring
natural blueberry extract (see Stockists, page 182), to taste
pink food colouring

For the chocolate tartlet shells

150g (5½oz/⅔ cup) unsalted butter, softened, plus extra for greasing
275g (9¾oz/2 cups) plain (all-purpose) flour, plus extra for dusting and flouring the tins
120g (4¼oz/¾ cup plus 2 tbsp) icing (confectioner's) sugar
2 medium eggs, at room temperature
½ tsp vanilla extract
25g (1oz/2 tbsp) cocoa powder
pinch of salt

For the blueberry custard

400g (14oz) Blueberry Purée (see page 179) made with 520g (18oz) fresh blueberries
100g (3½oz/½ cup) caster sugar
6 egg yolks
2 medium eggs
½ tsp pectin
150g (5½oz/⅔ cup) unsalted butter, softened

For the decoration

fresh edible violet or pansy blossoms
fresh lemon balm or mint leaves
fresh blueberries
dried edible rose petals

Specialist equipment (see page 164 for a basic equipment list and page 182 for stockists)

large piping bag fitted with a narrow star nozzle
large piping bag fitted with a large round nozzle
12 x 10cm (4in) round tartlet tins

TO MAKE THE BLUEBERRY MERINGUE KISSES

Preheat the oven to 80°C/175°F/Gas ¼.

Add a drop of blueberry extract to the meringue mixture.

Mix about 1 tbsp of the meringue with a drop of pink food colour and blend together with a palette knife until all the colour specks have dispersed. Add this back into the meringue and mix in until you have an even pastel shade.

Spoon half of the meringue into a large piping bag fitted with a narrow star nozzle. Spoon the other half into a large piping bag fitted with a large round nozzle.

Pipe round meringue kisses with the round nozzle onto a prepared baking tray – the bases should be just under 2cm (¾in). Pipe star-shaped meringue kisses with the star nozzle on another baking tray – with bases around 2.5cm (1in). The difference in size can be achieved by simply squeezing the bag for longer to increase the size.

Bake for about 1 hour, or until the meringues can be lifted clean off the tray. Allow to cool.

TO MAKE THE TARTLET SHELLS

Grease the tartlet tins with butter and lightly dust with flour. Chill the tins while you make the pastry.

Put the butter and icing sugar in the bowl of an electric mixer fitted with a paddle attachment and cream together until combined.

Add the eggs, one at a time, followed by the vanilla extract.

Sift together the flour, cocoa powder and salt. Slowly add it to the butter mix.

When the mix has come together, transfer the dough to a lightly floured, smooth work surface. Shape it into a ball and work it with your hands, stretching it and regathering it for a short while. This will work the gluten in the flour and toughen the dough slightly, which will make the tartlet shells crisper after baking. Wrap the dough in cling film and chill for 30 minutes.

Divide the dough into 10 even pieces and, one at a time, roll each out with a rolling pin on a lightly floured surface to a thickness of about 3–4mm (⅛in). Lay the pastry over the tartlet tins and gently push down the middle and sides using a small piece of dough. Trim the excess off using a kitchen knife. Prick the bases with a fork and chill for 20 minutes. Preheat the oven to 175°C fan/375°F/Gas 5.

Bake the pastry cases in the preheated oven for 10–12 minutes. Leave the tartlets to cool on a wire rack, then unmould from the tins when completely cool.

TO MAKE THE BLUEBERRY CUSTARD

Add half the sugar to the still hot blueberry purée and bring it back to a boil.

Put the remaining sugar and the pectin in a bowl and mix them together.

In a separate bowl, whisk the egg yolks and whole eggs together.

Add the sugar and pectin mix to the eggs and combine.

Pour the boiling blueberry purée onto the egg and sugar mixture and whisk to combine. Once combined, pour the mixture back into the saucepan and bring back to a gentle boil. Cook on a low heat for about 5 minutes while whisking constantly, until the mixture has thickened.

Remove the pan from the heat and transfer the custard to a bowl.

Place a sugar thermometer in the custard and cover as much of the top of the custard as possible with cling film to prevent a skin forming. Let it cool down to 59°C/138°F.

Once at the correct temperature, add the soft butter, a little at a time, while quickly whisking the custard to emulsify the mixture.

Use the blueberry custard to fill the tartlet shells to the top and level the tops off with a palette knife. Place in the fridge to cool.

TO DECORATE THE TARTLETS

Shortly before serving decorate each tartlet with one of each of the meringue kisses.

Garnish with fresh edible flowers, lemon balm or mint leaves, blueberries and dried rose petals.

Berries & 'Elderfleur' Cake

This beautiful floral cake has to be one of my favourite midsummer recipes. Light vanilla chiffon sponge is infused with elderflower syrup before being layered with elderflower buttercream, crushed berries and summer berry compote. The result is picturesque with an artful crown of bright berries and pretty petals.

MAKES A 15CM (6IN) CAKE (SERVES 10)

1 quantity Chiffon Sponge (3 x 15cm/6in cakes, see page 171) flavoured with 1 tsp vanilla extract

For the elderflower sugar syrup
100g (3½oz/½ cup) caster sugar
100ml (3½fl oz/scant ½ cup) water
15 drops elderflower extract (see Stockists, page 182)

For the mixed berry jam
150g (5½oz) Berry Purée (see page 179), made with 100g (3½oz) each of fresh strawberries, blueberries and raspberries
140g (5oz/¾ cup less 2 tsp) caster sugar
¼ tsp pectin

For the elderflower meringue buttercream
1 layer cake quantity Meringue Buttercream (see page 176)
15 drops of elderflower extract (see Stockists, page 182)

magenta food colouring paste (see Stockists, page 182)
2 tbsp freeze-dried raspberries, crushed

For the decoration
fresh raspberries
fresh blueberries
1 punnet fresh edible flowers (such as violets, pansies and cornflowers)
1 tbsp freeze-dried raspberries, crushed

Specialist equipment (see page 164 for a basic equipment list and page 182 for stockists)
3 x 15cm (6in) shallow cake tins
15cm (6in) thin cake board
small piping bag or make your own paper piping bag (see page 168)
bevelled buttercream comb
piping bag fitted with a small star nozzle (Wilton no.21)

TO MAKE THE ELDERFLOWER SUGAR SYRUP

Put the sugar and water in a saucepan, bring to a boil and cook until the sugar is dissolved. Remove from the heat and allow to cool.

Once cool, add the elderflower extract.

TO MAKE THE MIXED BERRY JAM

Heat the purée (or let it cool, if you have just made it) to 50°C/122°F.

Mix 20g (⅔oz/2 tbsp) of the sugar and the pectin together well until completely combined and add it to the hot berry purée. Bring to the boil with a sugar thermometer inside the mix.

Add the remaining sugar and continue to boil, while whisking, until the mixture reaches 103°C/217°F.

Pour the jam into a heatproof bowl and cover it with cling film to prevent a skin from forming.

Cool down slightly, then chill in the fridge.

TO MAKE THE ELDERFLOWER MERINGUE BUTTERCREAM

Once you have made the meringue buttercream, add the elderflower extract.

Mix 1 tbsp of the buttercream with a small amount of magenta food colouring to a dark pink shade and blend together with a palette knife until all the colour specks have dispersed.

Little by little, add the dark pink buttercream back to the batch and mix until you have reached a pastel purpley–pink shade.

TO ASSEMBLE AND DECORATE THE CAKE

With your baked chiffon sponge layers, follow the instructions for preparing the cake on page 172, up to the stage at which you've placed the first sponge layer on the cake board.

Using a palette knife, spread a layer of buttercream evenly on top of the sponge, about 5mm (¼in) thick. Sprinkle the crushed freeze-dried raspberries over the top.

Place the middle sponge layer on top (the one that has been trimmed on both sides) and soak it with the elderflower sugar syrup.

Spoon about 2 tbsp of the buttercream into a small piping bag and snip a small tip off the end. Pipe a 5mm (¼in) thick ring around the edge of the sponge layer. Fill the buttercream ring with the mixed berry jam using a spoon.

Place the third sponge on top, this time brown side up and brush the top with elderflower sugar syrup.

Ensure that all the sponges are centred and the top of the cake is level. Tidy up any bits of buttercream that are squeezing out from around the edges with a palette knife. Let the cake layers set in the fridge for about 20 minutes.

Place the cake back on the turntable. Coat the cake all around with more buttercream using a palette knife and side scraper. The first buttercream coat is also called a 'crumb coat' as its purpose is to hold the crumbs in place and create a solid basic shape. It doesn't have to be perfect and it's fine if some cake crumb shows through the buttercream.

Transfer the cake (including cake disc) back into the fridge and chill for at least 30 minutes, or until the buttercream has set.

Once cool, mask the cake with a perfectly smooth and even layer of buttercream. This time apply a slightly thicker coat of buttercream around the sides and use a bevelled buttercream comb to scrape around it (see page 52 for step-by-step photographs). Go around a few times if not perfect the first time. Transfer the cake back to the fridge and chill until the buttercream has set.

Decorate the cake no more than 2 hours before serving it otherwise the edible flowers may wilt. Spoon the remaining buttercream into a piping bag fitted with a small star nozzle. If the buttercream is too firm to pipe, gently warm it in the microwave before filling the piping bag with it.

Pipe a ring of 10 S-shaped scrolls, evenly spaced out, around the top of the cake

Arrange a mixture of fresh berries and edible flowers on top of the buttercream ring and sprinkle with crushed freeze-dried raspberries. Serve as soon as possible, or only add the edible flowers at the last minute.

Ombre Cherry & Chocolate

DRIP CAKE

This seasonal layer cake is a guaranteed showstopper and tastes just as scrumptious as it looks. A moist vanilla and chocolate chip sponge is layered with morello cherry jam and pink cherry meringue buttercream. If you're looking to perfect your 'drip cake' technique, this is the recipe for you.

MAKES A 15CM (6IN) CAKE (SERVES 10)

For the vanilla sugar syrup
75g (2½oz/⅓ cup) caster sugar
75ml (2½fl oz/⅓ cup) water
½ tsp vanilla extract

For the vanilla and chocolate chip sponge
125g (4½oz/½ cup) salted butter, softened
250g (9oz/1¼ cups) caster sugar
1 tsp vanilla extract
5 medium eggs
250g (9oz/1¾ cups plus 2 tbsp) self-raising flour, sifted
125g (4fl oz/½ cup) sunflower oil
100g (3½oz) dark chocolate chips (53% cocoa solids), roughly chopped

For the cherry meringue buttercream
125g (4½oz) Cherry Purée (see page 179), made from 400g (14oz) pitted fresh or frozen black morello cherries, cooled
1 layer cake quantity Meringue Buttercream (see page 176)
pink food colouring paste

For the morello cherry filling
150g (5½oz) good-quality morello cherry jam

For the chocolate ganache
75g (2½oz) dark chocolate (53% cocoa solids)
90ml (3fl oz/⅓ cup plus 1 tbsp) whipping cream
1 tsp liquid glucose

For the decoration
12 fresh cherries with stems

Specialist equipment (see page 164 for a basic equipment list and page 182 for stockists)
3 x 15cm/6in shallow cake tins
small piping bag, or make your own paper piping bag (see page 168)
15cm (6in) thin cake board
piping bag fitted with a small star nozzle

TO MAKE THE VANILLA SUGAR SYRUP

Put the sugar, water and vanilla extract in a saucepan, bring to a boil and cook until the sugar is dissolved. Remove from the heat and allow to cool.

TO MAKE THE VANILLA AND CHOCOLATE CHIP SPONGES

Preheat the oven to 175°C fan/375°F/Gas 5. Grease 3 x 15cm (6in) shallow cake tins with oil spray and line the bases with baking parchment.

Put the butter, sugar and vanilla extract into the bowl of an electric mixer fitted with a paddle attachment and beat at medium–high speed until pale and fluffy.

In a separate bowl, lightly beat the eggs, then slowly pour them into the butter and sugar mix while beating on medium speed. Watch as the eggs combine with the butter mix and stop pouring if the batter needs time to come together, then add more. The eggs and butter should both be at room temperature to avoid splitting. However, should the mixture split, add 1 tbsp flour to bring the batter back together before adding more egg.

Once all the eggs are incorporated, fold in the sifted flour in 2 batches, gently combining each time. Scrape the bottom of the bowl using a rubber spatula to ensure the batter is evenly mixed.

Add the oil and mix until combined.

Sprinkle the chocolate chips over the top and fold through.

Divide the batter evenly between the 3 prepared cake tins and gently spread the batter towards the edges. It should be slightly higher around the sides with a slight dip in the middle; this will ensure that it bakes evenly when it rises.

Bake in the preheated oven for 20–30 minutes. The sponges are cooked when the edges come away from the sides of the cake tin and the tops spring back to the touch.

Leave the sponges to rest in the tins for about 10 minutes then brush the tops with the vanilla sugar syrup while the cakes are still hot. This will prevent the cakes from forming a hard crust and ensure the moisture and flavour are absorbed evenly.

Once slightly cooled, unmould the sponges from the cake tins carefully without breaking the edges – use a small kitchen knife to release the sides if required. Leave to cool completely on a wire rack.

TO MAKE THE CHERRY MERINGUE BUTTERCREAM

Remove about one-third of the meringue buttercream from the main batch into a separate bowl and set aside for later.

Slowly fold in the cherry purée through the remaining two-thirds of the buttercream and gently mix until well combined. Ensure that the purée and buttercream are at the same room temperature to prevent the mixture from splitting.

TO ASSEMBLE THE CAKE

Start following the instructions for preparing the cake on page 172, up to the stage at which you've placed the first sponge layer on the cake board.

Spread a layer of cherry buttercream, about 5mm (¼in) thick, over the top of the first sponge using a palette knife.

Place the middle sponge on top. Spoon about 2 heaped tbsp of the buttercream into a small piping bag and snip a small tip off the end. Pipe a 5mm (¼in) thick ring around the edge of the sponge layer. Fill the buttercream ring with the cherry jam using a spoon.

Place the third sponge on top, this time brown side up.

Ensure that all the sponges are centred and the top of the cake is level. Tidy up any bits of buttercream that are squeezing out from around the edges with a palette knife.

Coat the cake all around with more buttercream using a palette knife and side scraper. The first buttercream coat is also called a 'crumb coat' as its purpose is to hold the crumbs in place and create a solid basic shape. It doesn't have to be perfect and it's fine if some cake crumb shows through the buttercream. Chill for about 30 minutes until the buttercream has set.

Divide the remaining cherry buttercream into 2 equal portions. Mix one half with a small amount of pink food colour to a deep cherry pink shade. You may wish to add a tiny bit of pink food colour to the pale pink buttercream as well to give it a little bit of a lift.

Once the crumb coat has set, place the cake back on the turntable and cover the top evenly with plain buttercream using the palette knife.

Apply 3 evenly-sized rings of dark pink, pale pink and plain buttercream around the sides, using the palette knife. (Alternatively, you can fill each colour into a piping bag and pipe rings around the sides instead of using the palette knife.)

Start at the bottom layer and spread the dark pink buttercream one-third of the way up the side of the cake. Follow suit with the pale pink buttercream for the middle third and finish with the plain buttercream for the upper third and the top of the cake. Reserve some pale pink cherry buttercream at room temperature for piping the rosettes later. See pages 26 and 27 for step-by-step photographs of creating ombre buttercream layers.

Smooth all 3 buttercream stripes using a side scraper. If not smooth after the first time, wipe the edge of the side scraper clean and go around again and again, until the sides look smooth. This time there should be no cake crumb visible.

Clean up the top edge of the cake by spreading the overhanging buttercream from the edge towards the middle of the cake using a palette knife or side scraper. Chill the cake again for about 1 hour.

TO MAKE THE CHOCOLATE GANACHE

Break the chocolate into pieces and place in a heatproof bowl. Gently heat the cream and liquid glucose in a small saucepan until steaming or just starting to simmer.

Pour the cream into the chocolate in 2 to 3 batches, mixing with a rubber spatula or whisk each time until combined.

Pour the ganache into a jug, cover the top with cling film to prevent a skin from forming and allow to cool for a few minutes until lukewarm.

TO DECORATE THE CAKE

Place the cake back on top of a turntable.

Pour the warm (not hot) ganache around the edge of the cake while turning it steadily. Allow the ganache to run down the edges in thin spaced out drips. If you find it easier, you can use a piping bag or sauce bottle instead of a jug for dripping.

Using a palette knife, spread the ganache towards the middle of the cake until it coats the whole top of the cake smoothly. Chill the cake for about 20 minutes, or until the ganache has set.

Spoon the remaining pale pink cherry buttercream into a piping bag fitted with a small star nozzle.

Pipe 10 evenly-sized and -spaced out rosettes around the top of the cake and stick a fresh cherry on top of each rosette.

Autumn & Halloween

The arrival of autumn is always a 'golden' time at the Parlours. A new energy can be felt as the skies glow with such a beautiful light, the leaves in Belgravia start to change colour and everything begins to feel that little bit cosier. Reminiscent of childhood, when this time of year was filled with shiny new school shoes and sharpened pencils, the Parlours get this same 'back to school' treatment with a fresh new look.

I always feel that autumn awakens the child in so many of us, as the delight of pumpkin picking and Halloween frivolity conjures up an air of nostalgic excitement. It's this unwritten understanding that allows us to really push boundaries with the Parlour's autumnal look and feel each year, ultimately giving permission for us to have great fun and be at our most daring.

In 2019, we transformed our Parlours overnight with a forest of giant toadstools. The utopian offering caused a huge wave of social media attention making it one of our most talked about collections yet. For this reason pumpkins and toadstools play a starring role in this chapter.

To really taste the beauty of this season, I am so happy to share our bestselling Spiced Pumpkin Cupcake recipe, as well as a Fancy Forager's Cupcake Trio, which really captures the flavours of this time of year. For Halloween, the Sweet Shivers Black Velvet Cake is the ultimate treat for all the family.

Pink Toadstool

CHAI—SPICED COOKIES

Baked with the warming aromas of autumnal chai spices, I always feel these fairy-tale pink toadstool cookies are almost too pretty to eat. The decorations may look elaborate, but when broken into stages the techniques used are straightforward and the tools I have suggested are very user friendly.

MAKES 12 COOKIES

For the chai-spiced cookie dough
1 quantity Basic Sugar Cookie Dough (see page 165), flavoured with these spices added with the flour:
2 tsp ground cinnamon
1 tsp ground ginger
1 tsp ground cardamom
½ tsp ground allspice
½ tsp ground cloves
plain (all-purpose) flour, for dusting

For the decoration
1 quantity Half & Half Paste (see page 166)
ivory, dusky pink and peppermint green food colouring pastes (see Stockists, page 182)
150g (5½oz) Royal Icing (see page 167)
icing (confectioner's) sugar and cornflour (cornstarch), for dusting

a small amount of white vegetable fat (eg Trex)
pearl edible lustre spray (see Stockists, page 182)
gold edible lustre dust (see Stockists, page 182)
a small amount of clear alcohol, such as vodka (alternatively use lemon juice)
50g (1¾oz) white sugar florist paste

Specialist equipment (see page 164 for a basic equipment list and page 182 for stockists)
medium and large toadstool cookie cutters (see Stockists, page 182, or instructions below and template on page 97)
medium and large gills stencil set (I had mine made by a stencil manufacturer – see Stockists, page 182, or instructions below and template on page 97)
rose stems silicone mould

TO MAKE THE COOKIES

Preheat the oven to 175°C fan/375°F/Gas 5 and line 2 baking trays with baking parchment.

To make your own cookie template, refer to the design on page 97. You will need one template actual size and one slightly larger, for 2 different sizes of toadstool. Trace or photocopy the outline, glue it onto a piece of card and cut it out. To make a gills stencil, trace or photocopy the area, place it on a thin piece of plastic (eg from a lid, or thick acetate) and cut the gill shapes out with a fine scalpel.

Unwrap the chilled cookie dough and briefly knead it through to soften it slightly. Place it onto a lightly floured work surface and roll it out to a thickness of about 5mm (¼in).

Using the toadstool cookie cutters, stamp out about 6 large and 6 medium cookies. If you've made templates, place them on the cookie dough and cut around them with a kitchen knife to make 6 cookies in each size. Place them onto the lined baking trays, spaced apart by at least 1cm (½in). Ensure that there are no wrinkles in the paper under the cookies and weigh the edges of the paper down if using a fan-assisted oven, otherwise the cookies may lift up during the baking process and turn out uneven. Put the trays in the fridge for about 10 minutes.

Bake in the preheated oven for 8–12 minutes, turning the trays once during baking to ensure they bake evenly. When cooked, they should look golden brown and spring back when you press down with your finger. Allow the cookies to cool on the trays.

TO DECORATE THE COOKIES

Divide the half & half paste into 3 equal pieces. Following the instructions for colouring on page 166, colour one portion of the paste to an ivory, one to a pale dusky pink and one to a slightly darker shade of dusky pink. Wrap each colour individually in cling film and leave to rest for about 10 minutes to allow the pastes to firm up slightly.

Mix the royal icing with a small amount of the dusky pink food colouring to a pale pink. Add a drop of water and mix it to a soft peak consistency (see page 167 for a guide to royal icing consistencies). Cover the icing with a damp cloth until ready to use.

Lightly dust a smooth surface or plastic board with cornflour and place the ivory paste on top. Apply a thin layer of vegetable fat to a rolling pin and roll the paste out to a thickness of 1mm (1/32in).

Place the gills stencil on top of the paste, allowing enough room around it for the toadstool cutter/template to fit, and thinly spread the gaps of the stencil with the pale pink royal icing using a mini palette knife. Scrape off any excess and spray the gills with the pearl edible lustre spray. Carefully lift the stencil off and clean it with a damp cloth before using it again.

Position the toadstool cutter/template over the gills and stamp out the toadstool shape. Place it onto a smooth surface that has been lightly dusted with icing sugar or cornflour and let it semi set.

Repeat the earlier instructions to prepare the icing for another 5 ivory toadstool cookies, and then change colour to the pale pink paste and do the

same for another 6 pink cookies. You can mix and match sizes as you wish.

Mix 1 tbsp white royal icing with 1 tsp water to make a sugar glue. Brush the top of each cookie thinly with the glue and stick the semi-set, stencilled toadstool on top.

Roll out the dark pink paste as described earlier. Cut out the toadstool caps using the upper part of the toadstool cutters and use a sharp kitchen knife to trim the caps just above the gills line.

Mix the gold edible lustre with a small amount of clear alcohol to make a thick liquid gold colour. Dip a flat artist's brush into the gold colour, hold it above the toadstool caps and flick the colour off the brush with your fingers until the caps are speckled.

Using the sugar glue, stick the correctly sized caps on the toadstools in contrasting colours.

Mix 40g (1½oz) of the sugar florist paste with a small amount of dusky pink food colouring to a dark dusky pink shade, and mix the remaining 10g (¼oz) of sugar florist paste with a small amount of peppermint green colouring. Add a dab of white vegetable fat if the pastes feel sticky.

Rub the inside of the rose silicone leaf mould with a thin layer of the vegetable fat. Cut the pink sugar florist paste into 12 evenly-sized pieces and roll each one into a smooth ball. One at a time, press each ball of paste into the rose mould, flatten the back and trim off any excess with a knife. Unmould by carefully bending the silicone mould outward until the rose drops out. You may want to grease the mould after each use.

Using the same technique as for the roses, make 12 to 18 green leaves using the single leaf part of the silicone mould.

Spray the roses and leaves lightly with the pearl edible lustre spray.

Stick one rose and 1–2 leaves on top of each cookie using royal icing. Allow to dry until completely set.

8.4CM (3⅓IN)

Spiced Pumpkin Cupcakes

Our favourite autumn cupcake flavour by far, each year we give the spiced pumpkin design a brand new look to reflect our seasonal theme. Our pink meringue toadstool decorations were designed for our 'Forage Fever' collection, our most talked about installation we've ever created at the Parlour.

MAKES 24 CUPCAKES

For the spiced cream cheese frosting
1 quantity Cream Cheese Frosting (see page 177)
2 tbsp ground cinnamon

For the meringue toadstools
2 quantities meringue (see Meringue Kisses, page 180)
  – follow the instructions up to the stage at which you're ready to add the flavouring
1 tsp vanilla extract
dusky pink food colouring paste (see Stockists, page 182)
2 tbsp white sugar pearls
cocoa powder, for dusting
200g (7oz) dark chocolate chips (53% cocoa solids), melted

For the pumpkin cupcakes
110g (3¾oz/½ cup less ¼ tbsp) unsalted butter
310g (11oz/1¼ cups) pumpkin purée
360g (12¾oz/1¾ cups plus 1 tbsp) light brown sugar
130g (4½oz/½ cup plus ½ tbsp) buttermilk
½ tsp salt
4 medium eggs
265g (9¼oz/2 cups) plain (all-purpose) flour
2½ tsp baking powder
generous ½ tsp bicarbonate of soda (baking soda)
2 tsp ground ginger
2¼ tsp ground cinnamon
pinch of ground cloves

To decorate
2 tbsp chopped pistachios

Specialist equipment (see page 164 for a basic equipment list and page 182 for stockists)
3 large piping bags each fitted with a 1cm (½in) round nozzle
2 x 12-hole cupcake trays
24 pink paper baking cases
large piping bag
large piping bag fitted with a large narrow star nozzle

TO MAKE THE SPICED CREAM CHEESE FROSTING

Prepare this well in advance, so it has time to chill. Once you have made the cream cheese frosting, add the cinnamon and stir well. Chill until needed.

TO MAKE THE MERINGUE TOADSTOOLS

Preheat the oven to 80°C/175°F/Gas ¼.

Add the vanilla extract to the meringue mixture and combine well.

Spoon half of the meringue into a large piping bag fitted with a 1cm (½in) round nozzle and set aside – this will remain white.

Mix about 1 tbsp of the remaining meringue with a drop of dusky pink food colouring and blend together with a palette knife until all the colour specks have dispersed and you have a medium pink.

Divide the remaining meringue equally between 2 bowls. Using a small amount of the pink meringue, colour one of the bowls a pale pink, adding the colour a little at a time until you reach the desired shade. Repeat with the other bowl, this time adding a little bit more of the coloured meringue so that you achieve a slightly darker shade of pink.

Spoon each meringue into separate large piping bags fitted with 1cm (½in) round nozzles.

Pipe about 30 small pale pink and 30 large dark pink toadstool caps on the lined baking trays. The small caps should have bases just under 2cm (¾in) wide and the large ones bases around 2.5cm (1in). You will need 48 toadstools for the cupcakes, but it's best to make a few extra in case of breakages.

Sprinkle the dark pink caps with the white sugar pearls, and dust the pale pink caps lightly with cocoa powder.

Using the piping bag with the white meringue, pipe about 30 small and 30 large toadstool stems. Start by piping a round blob and pull the bag up as you squeeze. When the stem is about 2.5cm (1in) tall, stop squeezing and pull up the bag so that the stem has a fine tip at the top. Dust the tips lightly with cocoa powder.

Bake for about 1 hour, or until the meringues can be lifted clean off the tray. Allow to cool.

To assemble the toadstools, dip the tip of a white stem into the melted chocolate and then push this into the base of a pink mushroom cap. Repeat until all the mushrooms have been assembled, ensuring that you match small stems with small caps, and the large stems with the large caps. Let the chocolate set completely.

TO MAKE THE PUMPKIN CUPCAKES

Preheat the oven to 175°C fan/375°F/Gas 5 and line the cupcake trays with the baking cases.

Melt the butter in a small saucepan and leave to cool slightly.

Put the pumpkin purée, sugar, buttermilk and salt in a bowl and mix together until fully combined.

In a separate bowl, lightly beat the eggs, then gradually add them to the mixture.

Sift the flour, baking powder, bicarbonate of soda and spices together and add them to the mixture in 3 batches, lightly mixing between additions.

Lastly, add the melted butter and gently mix until incorporated.

Fill a large piping bag with the batter and snip 2.5cm (1in) off the tip. Pipe the batter into the baking cases, filling each one about two-thirds full.

Bake in the preheated oven for about 15 minutes, depending on your oven. The cupcakes are cooked when the tops spring back to the touch and the edges of the baking cases have shrunk away from the sides of the baking tray.

Remove from the oven and leave to rest in the cupcake trays for a few minutes.

Transfer the cupcakes to a wire rack and leave to cool completely.

TO DECORATE THE CUPCAKES

Remove the cream cheese frosting from the fridge and give it a stir with a rubber spatula to soften it lightly.

Spoon the frosting into a piping bag fitted with a large narrow star nozzle and pipe a swirl of frosting on top of each cupcake.

Stick a large and a small toadstool into the frosting of each cupcake.

Sprinkle the chopped pistachios around the toadstool stems.

Decorate the cupcakes at the last minute and serve as soon as possible. Don't refrigerate the cakes for more than a couple of hours after the toadstools have been placed on top as the meringues will go soft and can melt or fall over.

TIP

If you have any leftover toadstools, they make lovely sweet gifts or treats as they will last for several weeks if stored in an airtight container somewhere cool.

Autumn & Halloween Style Secrets

When it comes to autumn and Halloween, pink is the new orange in my book, and this is the season for pink pumpkins galore. Each year, our expert florist Mathew Dickinson patiently paints what seems like a sea of pink pumpkins made from papier mâché. They need lots of coats of paint for the right shade of pink but the efforts are always well worth it. These pumpkin beauties also stand the test of time, and if you're creating the effect at home, you can reuse and build on your collection year on year.

When it comes to pumpkin colour and design, you can create a beautiful effect with a muted pastel colour scheme and the addition of a few vibrant accent colours. Shades of wine and mauve look striking with burnt orange and dusky pinks. There are several online suppliers – Etsy is a good place to look – where you can find fun vinyl stickers with Halloween phrases such as 'BOO!' or 'Trick or Treat'. These can be applied directly onto your pumpkins, adding a playful element to your chic display.

As well as paper pumpkins, you can also find paper autumn leaves, skull heads and skeletons online. While skulls and skeletons can be a little bit gruesome in white, spray paint them pastel and they suddenly look very stylish. I love to decorate them with silk flowers, diamanté jewels and pearls. You can find these at haberdashery suppliers, or the Covent Garden Flower Market in London is always a treasure trove.

For an inviting style with an eerie twist, incorporating antique-style lanterns into your floral display is really effective. Or for a bewitching look, source a traditional Besom broomstick and spray the tips with rose gold. As well as a decoration, it makes a great prop, and works well for a Halloween photobooth idea. Don't forget to bake some yummy pumpkin cookies for little (or big) trick-or-treaters and show off your baking skills with my Sweet Shivers Black Velvet Cake design (see page 125).

Fancy Forager's
CUPCAKE TRIO

Autumn has such an abundance of flavours to offer, you will feel spoilt for choice with these three seasonal recipes.

A classic autumnal favourite of mine are the Spiced Toffee Apple Cupcakes, made with a caramel buttermilk sponge and filled with apple compote, before being topped with a cinnamon cream cheese frosting and toffee sauce.

The Blackberry Crumble is a bounty of a cupcake. Blackberry buttermilk sponge is filled with blackberry jam and topped with a blackberry meringue buttercream, blackberry purée, fresh blackberry, oat crumble and offset with a touch of lemon balm.

The most sweet-toothed foragers can be satisfied with the Salted Caramel & Popcorn Cupcakes. Caramel buttermilk sponge is filled with sea salt toffee sauce, caramel cream cheese frosting and topped with crunchy sea-salt-caramel coated popcorn.

Spiced Toffee Apple Cupcakes

MAKES 24 CUPCAKES

For the cinnamon cream cheese frosting
1 quantity Cream Cheese Frosting (see page 177)
½ tsp vanilla extract
1 tsp ground cinnamon

For the vanilla sugar syrup
100g (3½oz/½ cup) caster sugar
100ml (3½fl oz/scant ½ cup) water
1 tsp vanilla extract

For the spiced apple cupcakes
110g (3¾oz/½ cup less ¼ tbsp) unsalted butter
pinch of salt
240g (8½oz/1¼ cups less 1 tbsp) caster sugar
145g (5oz/¾ cup less 1 tsp) light brown sugar
1 tsp ground cinnamon
3 eggs
270g (9½oz/2 cups) plain (all-purpose) flour
240g (8½oz/1 cup) buttermilk
1 tsp white wine vinegar
1 tsp bicarbonate of soda (baking soda)
180g (6¼oz) apples (golden delicious or granny smith), peeled and diced into small cubes

For the toffee sauce
100ml (3½fl oz/scant ½ cup) water

300g (10½oz/1½ cups) caster sugar
25g (¾oz/1½ tbsp) liquid glucose
200ml (7fl oz/scant 1 cup) double (heavy) cream
90g (3¼oz/6 tbsp) unsalted butter, diced
¾ tsp sea salt

For the apple compote
2 large apples (golden delicious or granny smith), peeled, cored and diced
a squeeze of lemon juice
drop of vanilla extract

For the decoration
24 large pearlescent pink choco balls (see Stockists, page 182)
Bordeaux glimmer 100s and 1000s (see Stockists, page 182)
pink metallic pearls, 4mm/⅛in (see Stockists, page 182)

Specialist equipment (see page 164 for a basic equipment list and page 182 for stockists)
2 x 12-hole cupcake baking trays
24 pink paper baking cases
large piping bag
large piping bag fitted with a large star nozzle

TO MAKE THE CINNAMON CREAM CHEESE FROSTING

Prepare this well in advance, so it has time to chill. Once you have made the cream cheese frosting, add the vanilla and the cinnamon and stir well to combine. Chill until needed.

TO MAKE THE VANILLA SUGAR SYRUP

Put the sugar, water and vanilla extract in a small saucepan and bring to a boil until the sugar has dissolved. Allow to cool.

TO MAKE THE SPICED APPLE CUPCAKES

Preheat the oven to 175°C fan/375°F/Gas 5 and line the cupcake trays with the baking cases.

Put the butter, salt, caster sugar, brown sugar and cinnamon in the bowl of an electric mixer fitted with a paddle attachment and cream together until pale and fluffy. This will take a while, so do this as a first step to allow plenty of time to aerate the mixture.

In a separate bowl, beat the eggs, then gradually add them to the butter mix, making sure the batter doesn't split. If it does split, add a small handful of flour to bring the mixture back together.

Alternating between the 2, add the flour and the buttermilk to the batter in batches and mix until combined.

Mix the vinegar and bicarbonate of soda together in a small bowl and immediately, as it bubbles up, add it to the batter.

Fill a large piping bag with the batter and snip 2.5cm (1in) off the tip. Pipe the batter into the baking cases, filling each one about two-thirds full.

Place 3–4 cubes of apple on top of the batter in each case; they will sink to the bottom during the baking process.

Bake in the preheated oven for about 15 minutes, depending on your oven. The cupcakes are cooked when they are golden, the tops spring back to the touch and the edges of the baking cases have shrunk away from the sides of the baking tray.

Remove from the oven and leave to rest in the cupcake trays for a few minutes.

Brush the tops of the cakes with the vanilla sugar syrup while still hot. This will ensure the sponges absorb the moisture and prevent a dry crust from forming.

Transfer the cupcakes to a wire rack and leave to cool completely. Wipe the bottoms with a damp cloth if sticky from the syrup. Do not leave the cupcakes to cool in the cupcake tray, as the cases may stick to the tray.

When cool, chill the cakes for 30 minutes to firm up the sponge.

TO MAKE THE TOFFEE SAUCE

Put the water, sugar and liquid glucose in a deep saucepan. Cook on a medium heat while stirring continuously until the sugar has melted and turned amber in colour.

Once the sugar has caramelised, carefully pour the cream into the caramel while stirring. The caramel will bubble up during this process so be careful.

Once the cream and the caramel are combined, add the butter and continue to stir for another 2–3 minutes until the butter is completely melted.

Let the mixture boil for about a minute, then remove the pan from the heat and stir in the sea salt.

Transfer to a bowl, cover the sauce with cling film and allow to cool completely.

TO COOK THE APPLE COMPOTE

Put the diced apples and the lemon juice in a saucepan and cook for about 5–10 minutes until you have a chunky compote.

Add the vanilla extract to taste and allow the compote to cool.

TO DECORATE THE CUPCAKES

Scoop a small well out of the centre of each cupcake using a melon baller.

Fill the centre of each cake with 1 tsp of the apple compote and 1 tsp of the toffee sauce. Reserve the remaining compote and sauce for later.

Remove the cream cheese frosting from the fridge and give it a stir with a rubber spatula to soften it slightly.

Spoon the frosting into a large piping bag fitted with a large star nozzle and pipe a swirl of frosting on top of each cupcake with a small well in the middle.

Spoon a small amount of apple compote into the well and drizzle with toffee sauce.

Decorate each cupcake with a large pearlescent pink choco balls, 100s and 1000s, and pink metallic pearls.

Serve as soon as possible or chill for about 30 minutes until the frosting has slightly set before transporting them. Always serve and enjoy at room temperature. The metallic pearls may melt if exposed to humidity and so should be added at the last minute.

Blackberry Crumble Cupcakes

For the blackberry jam filling

200g (7oz) fresh blackberries
squeeze of lemon juice
140g (5oz/¾ cup less 2 tsp) caster sugar
¼ tsp pectin

For the blackberry meringue buttercream

1 cupcake quantity Meringue Buttercream
  (see page 176)
250g (9oz) Blackberry Purée (see page 179), made
  from 500g (18oz) fresh blackberries, cooled

For the oat granola

100g (3½oz/1 cup) oats
1½ tsp honey
5 tsp sunflower oil
¼ tsp salt

For the vanilla sugar syrup

100g (3½oz/½ cup) caster sugar
100ml (3½fl oz/scant ½ cup) water
1 tsp vanilla extract

For the blackberry cupcakes

110g (3¾oz/½ cup less ¼ tbsp) unsalted butter
pinch of salt
240g (8½oz/1¼ cups less 1 tbsp) caster sugar
145g (5oz/¾ cup less 1 tsp) light brown sugar
3 eggs
1 tsp ground cinnamon
270g (9½oz/2 cups) plain (all-purpose) flour
240g (8½oz/1 cup) buttermilk
1 tsp white wine vinegar
1 tsp bicarbonate of soda (baking soda)
48 fresh blackberries (2 per cupcake)

For the decoration

24 fresh blackberries
24 fresh lemon balm leaves

**Specialist equipment (see page 164 for a basic
  equipment list and page 182 for stockists)**

2 x 12-hole cupcake baking trays
24 pink paper baking cases
large piping bag
large piping bag fitted with a large star nozzle

TO MAKE THE BLACKBERRY JAM FILLING

Put the blackberries and lemon juice in a saucepan
and cook until mushy. Let it cool to 50°C/122°F.

Mix 20g (⅔oz/2 tbsp) of the sugar and the pectin
together well until completely combined, then add
it to the warm blackberries and bring to the boil with
a sugar thermometer inside.

Add the remaining sugar and keep cooking,
whisking constantly, until the thermometer reaches
103°C/217°F.

Pour into a heatproof bowl and cover with cling film.
Allow to cool, then store in the fridge until later use.

TO MAKE THE BLACKBERRY MERINGUE BUTTERCREAM

Slowly add just half of the blackberry purée to the
meringue buttercream and mix until well combined.
(Reserve the rest of the purée for the cupcakes.)
Ensure that the purée and buttercream are at the
same room temperature to prevent the mixture
from splitting.

TO MAKE THE OAT GRANOLA

Preheat the oven to 175°C fan/375°F/Gas 5. Line a
baking tray with baking parchment.

Mix the oats together with the honey, oil and salt
and spread the mix out on the prepared tray.

Bake in the preheated oven for 10 minutes until golden brown.

Allow to cool, then wrap with cling film until needed.

TO MAKE THE VANILLA SUGAR SYRUP

Put the sugar, water and vanilla extract in a small saucepan and bring to a boil until the sugar has dissolved. Allow to cool.

TO MAKE THE BLACKBERRY CUPCAKES

Preheat the oven to 175°C fan/375°F/Gas 5 and line the cupcake trays with the baking cases.

Place the butter, salt, caster sugar and brown sugar into the bowl of an electric mixer fitted with a paddle attachment and cream together until pale and fluffy. This will take a while, so do this as a first step to allow plenty of time to aerate the mixture.

In a separate bowl, beat the eggs, then gradually add them to the butter mix, making sure the batter doesn't split. If it does split, add a small handful of flour to bring the mixture back together.

Combine the ground cinnamon with the flour in a bowl.

Alternating between the 2, add the flour and the buttermilk to the batter in batches and mix until combined.

In a small bowl, mix the vinegar and bicarbonate of soda together and immediately, as it bubbles up, add it to the batter.

Fill a large piping bag with the batter and snip 2.5cm (1in) off the tip. Pipe the batter into the baking cases, filling each one about two-thirds full.

Push 2 blackberries into the batter of each cupcake.

Bake in the preheated oven for about 15 minutes, depending on your oven. The cupcakes are cooked when they are golden, the tops spring back to the touch and the edges of the baking cases have shrunk away from the sides of the baking tray.

Remove from the oven and leave to rest in the cupcake trays for a few minutes.

Brush the tops of the cakes with the vanilla sugar syrup while still hot. This will ensure the sponges absorb the moisture and prevent a dry crust from forming.

Transfer the cupcakes to a wire rack and leave to cool completely. Wipe the bottoms with a damp cloth if sticky from the syrup. Do not leave the cupcakes to cool in the cupcake tray, as the cases may stick to the tray.

When cool, chill the cakes for 30 minutes to firm up the sponge.

TO DECORATE THE CUPCAKES

Scoop a small well out of the centre of each cupcake using a melon baller.

Using a teaspoon, fill the centres of the cakes with the blackberry jam.

Spoon the blackberry meringue buttercream into a large piping bag fitted with a large star nozzle. Pipe a generous rosette of buttercream on top of each cupcake.

Decorate each cake with a fresh blackberry, 1 tsp of the reserved blackberry purée, a sprinkle of oat granola and a lemon balm leaf.

Serve as soon as possible or chill for about 30 minutes until the buttercream has slightly set before transporting them. Always serve and enjoy at room temperature.

Salted Caramel & Popcorn Cupcakes

MAKES 24 CUPCAKES

For the salted caramel
100ml (3½fl oz/scant ½ cup) water
300g (10½oz/1½ cups) caster sugar
25g (¾oz/1½ tbsp) liquid glucose
200ml (7fl oz/scant 1 cup) double (heavy) cream
90g (3¼oz/6 tbsp) unsalted butter, diced
¾ tsp sea salt

For the caramel cream cheese frosting
250g (9oz/1 cup plus 2 tbsp) unsalted butter, softened
525g (1lb 2½oz/3⅓ cups) icing (confectioner's) sugar, sifted
250g (9oz/1 cup plus 2 tbsp) full-fat cream cheese, preferably Philadelphia

For the sea salt caramel popcorn
25g (1oz) popcorn kernels
1 tbsp vegetable oil
2 tsp sea salt
150g (5½oz/¾ cup) caster sugar

For the vanilla sugar syrup
75g (2½oz/⅓ cup) caster sugar
75ml (2½fl oz/⅓ cup) water
1 tsp vanilla extract

For the caramel cupcakes
110g (3¾oz/½ cup less ¼ tbsp) unsalted butter
240g (8½oz/1¼ cups less 1 tbsp) caster sugar
145g (5oz/¾ cup less 1 tsp) dark brown sugar
3 eggs
270g (9½oz/2 cups) plain (all-purpose) flour
240g (8½oz/1 cup) buttermilk
1 tsp white wine vinegar
1 tsp bicarbonate of soda (baking soda)

Specialist equipment (see page 164 for a basic equipment list and page 182 for stockists)
2 x 12-hole cupcake baking trays
24 gold metallic baking cases
large piping bag
large piping bag fitted with a large star nozzle

TO MAKE THE SALTED CARAMEL

Put the water, sugar and liquid glucose in a deep saucepan. Cook on a medium heat while stirring continuously until the sugar has melted and turned amber in colour.

Once the sugar has caramelised, carefully pour the cream into the caramel while stirring. The caramel will bubble up during this process so be careful.

Once the cream and the caramel are combined, add the butter and continue to stir for another 2–3 minutes until the butter is completely melted.

Let the mixture boil for about a minute, then remove the pan from the heat and stir in the sea salt.

Transfer to a bowl, cover the sauce with cling film and allow to cool completely.

TO MAKE THE CARAMEL CREAM CHEESE FROSTING

Prepare this well in advance, so it has time to chill.

Cream the butter and icing sugar together until pale and fluffy.

Soften the cream cheese with a spatula and mix until smooth. Add it to the butter mixture in batches and beat until smooth and well combined.

Add 150g (5½oz) of the cold salted caramel you made earlier and mix until combined. Reserve the remainder for later.

Cover the frosting with cling film and chill for later.

TO MAKE THE SEA SALT CARAMEL POPCORN

Heat the oil in a large saucepan on a medium heat with a couple of corn kernels inside.

Toss the remaining corn in a small amount of oil.

When the corn in the pan starts to pop, add the rest of the corn and cover with a lid. Continue to heat, shaking the pan frequently to prevent the corn from overheating, until all the kernels have popped. Transfer the popped corn to a bowl (removing any unpopped kernels as you go) and allow to cool.

Sprinkle the popcorn with the sea salt and mix well.

Put the sugar in a saucepan and heat until it starts to melt. Heat until the melted sugar turns amber, stirring constantly, then turn off the heat.

Pour the warm caramel over the popcorn and coat the popcorn well with the caramel using a spatula or spoon. Spread the popcorn out on a sheet of baking parchment and allow it to cool.

Break the popcorn into small chunks and store in an airtight container until needed.

TO MAKE THE VANILLA SUGAR SYRUP

Put the sugar, water and vanilla extract in a small saucepan and bring to a boil until the sugar has dissolved. Allow to cool.

TO MAKE THE CARAMEL CUPCAKES

Preheat the oven to 175°C fan/375°F/Gas 5 and line the cupcake trays with the baking cases.

Put the butter, salt and both sugars into the bowl of an electric mixer fitted with a paddle attachment and cream together until pale and fluffy. This will take a while, so do this as a first step to allow plenty of time to aerate the mixture.

In a separate bowl, beat the eggs, then gradually add them to the butter mix, making sure the batter doesn't split. If it does split, add a small handful of flour to bring the mixture back together.

Alternating between the 2, add the flour and the buttermilk to the batter in batches. Mix to combine.

Mix the vinegar and bicarbonate of soda together and immediately, as it bubbles up, add to the batter.

Fill a large piping bag with the batter and snip 2.5cm (1in) off the tip. Pipe the batter into the baking cases, filling each one about two-thirds full. Start in the centre of the base of the case, then move the piping bag up and around the outside of the case, leaving a dip in the middle; this will ensure that the cupcakes rise more evenly.

Bake in the preheated oven for about 15 minutes, depending on your oven. The cupcakes are cooked when they are golden, the tops spring back to the touch and the edges of the baking cases have shrunk away from the sides of the baking tray.

Remove from the oven and leave to rest in the cupcake trays for a few minutes.

Brush the tops of the cakes with the sugar syrup while still hot. This will ensure the sponges absorb the moisture and prevent a dry crust from forming.

Transfer the cupcakes to a wire rack and leave to cool completely. Wipe the bottoms with a damp cloth if sticky from the syrup. Do not leave the cupcakes to cool in the cupcake tray, as the cases may stick to the tray.

When cool, chill the cakes for 30 minutes to firm up.

TO DECORATE THE CUPCAKES

Scoop a small well out of the centre of each cupcake using a melon baller. Fill the centre with 1 tsp salted caramel.

Remove the cream cheese frosting from the fridge and give it a stir to soften it slightly.

Spoon the frosting into a large piping bag fitted with a large star nozzle and pipe a rosette of caramel cream cheese frosting on top of each cupcake.

Reheat the caramel to make it runny again (but not hot) if necessary. Drizzle it over the frosting and decorate with the chunks of caramel popcorn.

Serve as soon as possible or chill for about 30 minutes until the buttercream has slightly set before transporting them. Always serve and enjoy at room temperature.

Blackberry & Pear Cake

Taking inspiration from nature's larder, I adore this scrumptious combination of seasonal pear and blackberry sponge layered with a smooth blackberry meringue buttercream and topped with fresh blackberries. It's always a very satisfying way to round off an invigorating autumnal walk.

MAKES A 15CM (6IN) CAKE (SERVES 10)

For the vanilla sugar syrup
75g (2½oz/⅓ cup) caster sugar
75ml (2½fl oz/⅓ cup) water
½ tsp vanilla extract

For the blackberry, pear and buttermilk sponge
65g (2¼oz/¼ cup) unsalted butter
65g (2¼oz/¼ cup) salted butter
330g (11½oz/1¾ cups less 2 tbsp) caster sugar
1 tsp vanilla extract
1 egg
300g (10½oz/2¼ cups) plain (all-purpose) flour
300g (10½oz/1¼ cups) buttermilk
1½ tsp bicarbonate of soda (baking soda)
1½ tsp white wine vinegar
100g (3½oz) frozen or fresh blackberries
1 fresh pear, peeled, cored and diced

For the blackberry meringue buttercream
80g (2¾oz) Blackberry Purée (see page 179), made from 160g (5½oz) fresh blackberries, cooled
1 layer cake quantity Meringue Buttercream (see page 176)
magenta food colouring paste

For the decoration
1 tbsp freeze-dried blackberries
10 fresh blackberries

Specialist equipment (see page 164 for a basic equipment list and page 182 for stockists)
3 x 15cm (6in) shallow cake tins
15cm (6in) thin cake board
piping bag fitted with a narrow star nozzle

TO MAKE THE VANILLA SUGAR SYRUP

Put the sugar, water and vanilla extract in a saucepan, bring to a boil and cook until the sugar is dissolved. Remove from the heat and allow to cool.

TO MAKE THE BLACKBERRY, PEAR AND BUTTERMILK SPONGE LAYERS

Preheat the oven to 175°C fan/375°F/Gas 5. Grease 3 x 15cm (6in) shallow cake tins with oil spray and line the bases with baking parchment.

Put both butters, the sugar and the vanilla extract into the bowl of an electric mixer fitted with a paddle attachment and cream together until pale and fluffy. This will take a while, so do this as a first step to allow plenty of time to aerate the mixture.

In a separate bowl, lightly beat the eggs, then slowly pour them into the butter and sugar mix while beating on medium speed. Watch as the eggs combine with the butter mix and stop pouring if the batter needs time to come together, then add more. The eggs and butter should both be at room temperature to avoid splitting. However, should the mixture split, add 1 tbsp flour to bring the batter back together before adding more egg.

Alternating between the 2, add the flour and the buttermilk to the batter in batches and mix until combined.

In a small bowl, mix the vinegar and bicarbonate of soda together and immediately, as it bubbles up, add it to the batter.

Divide the batter evenly between the 3 prepared cake tins and and sprinkle the frozen blackberries and diced pear on top.

Bake in the preheated oven for 20–30 minutes. The sponges are cooked when the edges come away from the sides of the cake tin and the tops spring back to the touch.

Leave the sponges to rest in the tins for about 10 minutes and brush the tops with the sugar syrup while the cakes are still hot. This will prevent the cakes from forming a hard crust and the heat will ensure the moisture and flavour are absorbed evenly. Reserve the remainder of the syrup for layering.

Once slightly cooled, unmould the sponges from the cake tins carefully without breaking the edges – use a small kitchen knife to release the sides if required. Leave to cool completely on a wire rack.

TO MAKE THE BLACKBERRY MERINGUE BUTTERCREAM

Slowly fold the blackberry purée through the meringue buttercream in 3 batches and gently mix until well combined. Ensure that the purée and buttercream are at the same room temperature to prevent the mixture from splitting.

TO ASSEMBLE AND DECORATE THE CAKE

Layer and crumb coat the sponge layers using the blackberry buttercream as per the instructions on page 172, but omitting the instructions about brushing the sponges with sugar syrup.

Remove one-third of the remaining blackberry buttercream to a separate bowl. Mix 1 tbsp of that buttercream with some magenta food colouring to a deep purple shade and blend together with a palette knife until all the colour specks have dispersed. Little by little, add the purple buttercream back to the batch and mix until you have reached a dark purple shade. You may wish to add a little food colour to the pale blackberry buttercream as well to give it a lift.

Once the crumb coat has set, place the cake back on the turntable and cover the top evenly with pale purple blackberry buttercream using a palette knife.

Apply a ring of dark purple buttercream around the bottom third of the cake. You can either use a palette knife to spread the buttercream around, or you may find it easier to use a piping bag and pipe a ring around the side.

Cover the upper two-thirds of the cake with the pale blackberry buttercream. Reserve any remaining pale blackberry buttercream at room temperature for piping the rosettes later.

Smoothen the sides using a side scraper. If not smooth after the first time, wipe the edge of the side scraper clean and go around again and again, until they look smooth.

Clean up the top edge of the cake by spreading the overhanging buttercream from the edge towards the middle of the cake using a palette knife or side scraper. Chill the cake again for about 1 hour.

Crush the freeze-dried blackberries and dust over the centre of the cake using a sieve.

Spoon the remaining pale purple buttercream into a piping bag fitted with a narrow star nozzle.

Pipe 10 evenly-sized and -spaced out rosettes around the top of the cake using the purple buttercream and stick a blackberry on top of each rosette.

Pink Pumpkin Cookies

Trick-or-treaters will relish this playful pink pumpkin design. Ideal for a child-friendly bake, a vanilla cookie base is iced with pink sugar paste and decorated with a black jack-o'-lantern face. The clever use of a stencil ensures a simple yet impressive result.

MAKES ABOUT 12 COOKIES

For the cookies

1 quantity Basic Sugar Cookie Dough (see page 165) flavoured with 1 tsp vanilla extract
plain (all-purpose) flour, for dusting

For the decoration

1 quantity Half & Half Paste (see page 166)
fuchsia pink food colouring paste (see Stockists, page 182)
a small amount of white vegetable fat (eg Trex)
150g (5½oz) Royal Icing, soft peak consistency (see page 167)

black food colouring paste
icing (confectioner's) sugar and cornflour (cornstarch), for dusting
pearl edible lustre spray (see Stockists, page 182)

Specialist equipment (see page 164 for a basic equipment list and page 182 for stockists)

large pumpkin-shaped cookie cutter (about 12cm/ 4½in wide)
Dresden or veining tool
pumpkin face stencil

TO MAKE THE COOKIES

Preheat the oven to 175°C fan/375°F/Gas 5 and line 2 baking trays with baking parchment.

Unwrap the chilled cookie dough and briefly knead it through to soften it slightly.

Place the dough onto a lightly floured work surface and roll it out to an even thickness of about 5mm (¼in).

Using the pumpkin cookie cutter, stamp out about 12 cookies and place them onto the lined baking trays, spaced apart by at least 1cm (½in). Ensure that there are no wrinkles in the paper under the cookies and weigh the edges of the paper down if using a fan-assisted oven, otherwise the cookies may lift up during the baking process and turn out uneven. Put the trays of cookies in the fridge to chill for about 10 minutes.

Bake in the preheated oven for 8–12 minutes, turning the trays once during baking to ensure they bake evenly. When cooked, they should look golden brown and spring back when pressing down with your finger. Allow the cookies to cool on the trays.

TO DECORATE THE COOKIES

Following the instructions for colouring on page 166, use fuchsia pink food colouring to colour the half & half paste to a bright shade of pink. Wrap in cling film and rest for about 10 minutes to allow it to firm up slightly.

Mix 120g (4¼oz) of the royal icing with some black food colouring to a deep black. Add a drop of water and mix it to a soft peak consistency (see page 167 for a guide to royal icing consistencies). Cover the icing with a damp cloth until ready to use.

Lightly dust a smooth surface or plastic board with cornflour and place the pink paste on top. Apply a thin layer of vegetable fat to a rolling pin and roll the paste out to a thickness of 1mm (¹⁄₃₂in).

Using the pumpkin cutter, stamp out 12 pieces. Using the Dresden/veining tool, emboss each one with lines to look like grooves. Run the tool from the pumpkin bottom going up and from the top going down, each time gradually lifting off as you draw the lines.

Place the pumpkin face stencil on top of the pumpkin shapes and spread the eyes and mouth thinly with the black royal icing using a small palette knife. Scrape off any excess icing and peel the stencil off. Wipe the stencil clean with a damp cloth before using it again, dry it, then repeat for the remaining pumpkins.

Lightly spray the pumpkins with the pearl edible lustre spray to give them a light shimmer.

Mix the remaining white royal icing with enough water to make a sugar glue. Brush each cookie thinly with the glue and place a pink sugar pumpkin on top. Gently press down the edges while the paste is still pliable and allow to dry.

Black Velvet Cupcakes

BOO! This cute cupcake always gives the sweetest of shivers. An adorable sugar ghost lurks on top of a black velvet sponge with pink vanilla cream cheese frosting, meringue kisses and sprinkles. For those of you who love sugar crafting, I've given you detailed step-by-step instructions on how to make the sugar ghosts. However, you will find ready-made versions online if you prefer to skip that part of the recipe.

MAKES 24 CUPCAKES

For the sugar ghosts

150g (5½oz) white sugar florist paste
icing (confectioner's) sugar and cornflour (cornstarch), for dusting
a small amount of white vegetable fat (eg Trex)
black edible food pen (see Stockists, page 182)
pearl edible lustre spray (see Stockists, page 182)

For the pink vanilla cream cheese frosting

1 quantity Cream Cheese Frosting (see page 177)
1 tsp vanilla extract
fuchsia pink food colouring paste (see Stockists, page 182)

For the meringue kisses

1 quantity Meringue Kisses (see page 180) – follow the instructions up to the stage at which you're ready to add the flavouring
1 tsp vanilla extract
fuchsia pink food colouring paste

For the vanilla sugar syrup

150g (5½oz/¾ cup) caster sugar
150ml (5fl oz/scant ⅔ cup) water
1 tsp vanilla extract

For the black velvet cupcakes

130g (4¾oz/½ cup plus 1 tbsp) salted butter, softened
330g (11½oz/1½ cups plus 2 tbsp) caster sugar
1 tsp vanilla extract
2 large eggs, at room temperature
2 tbsp activated charcoal
300g (10½oz/1¼ cups) buttermilk
280g (10oz/2 cups plus 2 tbsp) plain (all-purpose) flour, sifted
25g (1oz/¼ cup) cocoa powder
1½ tsp white wine vinegar
1 tsp bicarbonate of soda (baking soda)

For the decorations

silver star sprinkles (see Stockists, page 182)
silver macaroni rods (see Stockists, page 182)
pink glimmer vermicelli (see Stockists, page 182)
pink and silver mini sugar pearls (see Stockists, page 182)

Specialist equipment (see page 164 for a basic equipment list and page 182 for stockists)

mini ghost cutter
large piping bag fitted with a 1cm (½in) round nozzle
large piping bag
2 x 12-hole cupcake trays
24 pink metallic baking cases
2 large piping bags each fitted with a large star nozzle

TO MAKE THE SUGAR GHOSTS

Mix the sugar florist paste with a small amount of vegetable fat to a smooth, pliable paste. Remove any dry and brittle pieces of paste before kneading it, as it will spoil the batch and look lumpy.

Lightly dust a smooth surface or plastic board with cornflour and place the white sugar florist paste on top. Apply a thin layer of vegetable fat to a rolling pin and roll the paste out to a thickness of 1mm (1⁄32in).

Using the mini ghost cutter, stamp out 24 ghosts (plus a few extra in case of breakages). Leave them to dry on a smooth surface that has been lightly dusted with icing sugar or cornflour. This may take at least 4 hours or ideally overnight.

Once dry, draw little faces on each ghost using the black food pen. Have some fun by varying the expressions.

Once the edible ink is dry, spray the ghosts with the pearl edible lustre spray.

TO MAKE THE MERINGUE KISSES

Preheat the oven to 80°C/175°F/Gas ¼.

Add the vanilla extract to the meringue mixture.

Spoon two-thirds of the meringue into a piping bag fitted with a large star nozzle and set aside – this will stay white.

Mix about 1 tbsp of the remaining meringue with a drop of fuchsia pink food colouring and blend together with a palette knife until all the colour specks have dispersed. Add this back into the meringue, a little at a time, and mix in until you have an even pink shade.

Spoon the pink meringue into the piping bag with the 1cm (½in) round nozzle. Pipe 30 round kisses onto the prepared tray – the bases should be about 1.5cm (just over ½in).

Using the piping bag with the white meringue, pipe about 30 larger kisses – the bases should be just under 2cm (¾in).

Bake for about 1 hour, or until the meringues can be lifted clean off the tray. Allow to cool.

TO MAKE THE PINK VANILLA CREAM CHEESE FROSTING

Prepare this well in advance, so it has time to chill. Once you have made the cream cheese frosting, add the vanilla and mix in well.

Mix about 1 tbsp of the frosting with a drop of fuchsia pink food colour and blend together with a palette knife until all the colour specks have dispersed and you have a deep pink shade. Add the coloured frosting, a little at a time, back into the white batch and mix until you get an even pink colour.

Cover the bowl with either a lid or cling film and chill until ready to use.

TO MAKE THE VANILLA SUGAR SYRUP

Put the sugar, water and vanilla extract in a small saucepan and bring to a boil until the sugar has dissolved. Allow to cool.

TO MAKE THE BLACK VELVET CUPCAKES

Preheat the oven to 175°C fan/375°F/Gas 5 and line the cupcake trays with the baking cases.

Put the butter, sugar and vanilla extract in the bowl of an electric mixer fitted with a paddle attachment and cream together until pale and fluffy. This will take a while, so do this as a first step to allow plenty of time to aerate the mixture.

Beat the eggs in a separate bowl, then add them to the butter mix, a little at a time, beating well between additions and making sure the batter doesn't split.

In another bowl, mix the activated charcoal with the buttermilk.

Mix the flour and cocoa powder in a separate bowl.

Alternating between the 2, add the flour and the buttermilk to the batter in batches and mix until combined.

Mix the vinegar and bicarbonate of soda together in a small bowl and immediately, as it bubbles up, add it to the batter.

Fill a large piping bag with the batter and snip 2.5cm (1in) off the tip. Pipe the batter into the baking cases, filling each one about two-thirds full. Start in the centre of the base of the case, then move the piping bag up and around the outside of the case, leaving a dip in the middle; this will ensure that the cupcakes rise more evenly.

Bake in the preheated oven for about 15 minutes, depending on your oven. The cupcakes are cooked when the tops spring back to the touch and the edges of the baking cases have shrunk away from the sides of the baking tray.

Remove from the oven and leave to rest in the cupcake trays for a few minutes.

Brush the tops of the cakes with the vanilla sugar syrup while still hot. This will ensure the sponges absorb the moisture and prevent a dry crust from forming.

Transfer the cupcakes to a wire rack and leave to cool completely. Wipe the bottoms with a damp cloth if sticky from the syrup. Do not leave the cupcakes to cool in the cupcake tray, as the cases may stick to the tray.

TO DECORATE THE CUPCAKES

Remove the cream cheese frosting from the fridge and give it a stir with a rubber spatula to soften it slightly.

Spoon it into a piping bag fitted with a large star nozzle and pipe a rosette of frosting on top of each cupcake.

Decorate each cupcake with a sugar ghost, a couple of meringue kisses and some star sprinkles, macaroni rods, glimmer vermicellli and mini sugar pearls.

Serve as soon as possible or chill for about 30 minutes until the frosting has slightly set before transporting them. Always serve and enjoy at room temperature. The sugar ghosts and meringues may melt if exposed to humidity and should be consumed within 24 hours once placed on a cupcake.

Sweet Shivers

BLACK VELVET CAKE

Be the 'hostess with the mostess' and captivate your guests with this spellbinding layer cake design. Bite through the white marshmallow spun cobwebs and pink vanilla buttercream, into sumptuous layers of black velvet sponge and pink vanilla cream cheese frosting. Cheeky ghost characters, meringue kisses, and sprinkles will complete your Halloween-themed party cake. For a perfectly pink Halloween display, why not pair with the Black Velvet Cupcakes (page 121) and Pink Pumpkin Cookies (page 117)?

MAKES A 15CM (6IN) CAKE (SERVES 10)

For the sugar ghosts

120g (4¼oz) white sugar florist paste
a small amount of white vegetable fat (eg Trex)
fuchsia pink food colouring paste (see Stockists, page 182)
icing (confectioner's) sugar and cornflour (cornstarch), for dusting
black edible food pen (see Stockists, page 182)
edible blush pink blossom tint (see Stockists, page 182)
pearl edible lustre spray (see Stockists, page 182)

For the meringue kisses

1 quantity Meringue Kisses (see page 180) – follow the instructions up to the stage at which you're ready to add the flavouring
1 tsp vanilla extract
fuchsia pink food colouring paste

For the vanilla sugar syrup

75g (2½oz/⅓ cup) caster sugar
75ml (2½fl oz/⅓ cup) water
½ tsp vanilla extract

For the black velvet sponge

105g (3½oz/7 tbsp) salted butter
265g (9¼oz/1¼ cups plus 1½ tbsp) caster sugar
1 tsp vanilla extract
2 eggs
1½ tbsp activated charcoal
240g (8½oz/1 cup) buttermilk
225g (8oz/1¾ cups) plain (all-purpose) flour, sifted
20g (⅔oz/3 tbsp) cocoa powder
1 tsp white wine vinegar
1 tsp bicarbonate of soda (baking soda)

For the vanilla cream cheese filling

100g (3½oz/scant ½ cup) full-fat cream cheese, preferably Philadelphia
100g (3½oz/7 tbsp) unsalted butter, softened
200g (7oz/1½ cups less 1 tbsp) icing (confectioner's) sugar, sifted
½ tsp vanilla extract
fuchsia pink food colouring paste

For the pink vanilla meringue buttercream

45ml (3 tbsp) water
190g (scant 1 cup) caster sugar
105g (3½ oz) egg whites (from approx. 5 eggs)
240g (9oz/1 cup plus 1 tbsp) unsalted butter, diced and softened
½ tsp vanilla extract
fuchsia pink food paste colouring

For the decorations

300g (10oz) marshmallows
silver star sprinkles (see Stockists, page 182)
silver macaroni rods (see Stockists, page 182)
pink glimmer vermicelli (see Stockists, page 182)
pink and silver mini sugar pearls (see Stockists, page 182)
mini marshmallows

Specialist equipment (see page 164 for a basic equipment list and page 182 for stockists)

'BOO' lettering stamps
ghost cookie cutter set
large piping bag fitted with a 1cm (½in) round nozzle
large piping bag fitted with a star nozzle
3 x 15cm (6in) round shallow cake tins
15cm (6in) round thin cake board
rubber gloves

TO MAKE THE SUGAR GHOSTS

Mix the sugar florist paste with a small amount of vegetable fat to a smooth, pliable paste. Remove any dry and brittle pieces of paste before kneading it, as it will spoil the batch and look lumpy.

Mix about one-third of the paste with a small amount of fuchsia food colouring to a medium pink shade and wrap in cling film.

Lightly dust a smooth surface or plastic board with cornflour and place the white sugar florist paste on top. Apply a thin layer of vegetable fat to a rolling pin and roll the paste out to a thickness of 1mm (1/32in).

For the large white ghost, press the BOO letters into the middle of the paste until the letters show in the icing.

Place the large ghost cutter on the paste with the BOO sitting centred on the upper belly and stamp it out.

Re-roll the paste and stamp out 2 to 3 small white ghosts using the smallest cookie cutter.

Repeat the rolling and cutting process for about another 3 small ghosts using the pink sugar florist paste.

Transfer the sugar ghosts onto a smooth surface that has been lightly dusted with icing sugar or cornflour and let them dry completely. This may take at least 4 hours, or ideally overnight.

Once dry, paint little faces on each of the ghosts using the black edible food pen. Have some fun by varying the facial expressions.

Add little pink cheeks using the blush pink blossom tint and a fine artist's brush.

Spray the ghosts with the pearl edible lustre spray.

TO MAKE THE MERINGUE KISSES

Preheat the oven to 80°C/175°F/Gas ¼.

Add the vanilla extract to the meringue mixture and stir well to combine.

Divide the meringue into 2 equal portions and set one aside – this will stay white.

Mix about 1 tbsp of the remaining meringue with a drop of fuchsia pink colour and blend together with a palette knife until all the colour specks have dispersed. Add this back into the meringue and mix in until you have an even pink shade.

Using a large piping bag fitted with a 1cm (½in) round nozzle and another piping bag fitted with a star nozzle, pipe a selection of differently-sized pink and white meringue kisses on the prepared trays. The sizes should range from about 8mm (⅓in) to 2.2cm (1in) – the difference in size can be achieved by simply squeezing the bag for longer to increase the size.

You may end up with more meringues than you need to decorate the cake, but you can use them either as additional confectionery on your table, displayed in a candy jar for example, or store them in an airtight container for up to 6 weeks and use them for a dessert.

Bake for about 1 hour, or until the meringues can be lifted clean off the tray. Allow to cool.

TO MAKE THE VANILLA SUGAR SYRUP

Put the sugar, water and vanilla extract in a saucepan, bring to a boil and cook until the sugar is dissolved. Remove from the heat and allow to cool.

TO MAKE THE BLACK VELVET SPONGE LAYERS

Preheat the oven to 175°C fan/375°F/Gas 5. Grease 3 x 15cm (6in) shallow cake tins with oil spray and line the bases with baking parchment.

Put the butter, sugar and vanilla extract into the bowl of an electric mixer fitted with a paddle attachment and beat at medium–high speed until pale and fluffy. This will take a while, so do this as a first step to allow plenty of time to aerate the mixture.

In a bowl, lightly beat the eggs, then slowly pour them into the butter and sugar mix while beating on medium speed. Watch as the eggs combine with the butter mix and stop pouring if the batter needs time to come together, then add more. The eggs and butter should both be at room temperature to avoid splitting. However, should the mixture split, add 1 tbsp flour to bring the batter back together before adding more egg.

Mix the activated charcoal with the buttermilk in a small bowl.

Mix the flour and cocoa powder in a separate bowl.

Alternating between the 2, add the flour and the buttermilk to the batter in batches and mix until combined.

Mix the vinegar and bicarbonate of soda together and immediately, as it bubbles up, add it to the batter.

Divide the batter evenly between the 3 prepared cake tins and gently spread the batter towards the edges.

Bake in the preheated oven for 20–30 minutes. The sponges are cooked when the edges come away from the sides of the cake tin and the tops spring back to the touch.

Leave the sponges to rest in the tins for about 10–15 minutes and brush the tops with the sugar syrup. This will prevent the cakes from forming a hard crust and the heat will ensure the moisture and flavour are absorbed evenly. Reserve the remainder of the syrup for layering.

Once slightly cooled, unmould the sponges from the cake tins carefully without breaking the edges – use a small kitchen knife to release the sides if required. Leave to cool completely on a wire rack.

TO MAKE THE VANILLA CREAM CHEESE FILLING

Make the cream cheese filling following the instructions on page 177, but using the quantities listed in this recipe on page 125.

Add the vanilla extract and mix in well.

Mix 1 tbsp vanilla cream cheese filling with some fuchsia pink food colouring to a deep pink shade and blend together with a palette knife until all the colour specks have dispersed.

Little by little, add the pink filling back to the main batch and mix until you have reached a medium shade of pink.

Cover the bowl with either a lid or cling film and chill until ready to use.

TO MAKE THE PINK VANILLA MERINGUE BUTTERCREAM

Make the meringue buttercream following the instructions on page 176, but using the quantities listed in this recipe on page 125.

Add the vanilla extract and mix until combined.

Mix 1 tbsp of the buttercream with a small amount of fuchsia pink food colouring to a dark pink shade and blend together with a palette knife until all the colour specks have dispersed.

Little by little, add the dark pink buttercream back to the main batch and mix until you have reached a medium pink shade.

TO ASSEMBLE AND DECORATE THE CAKE

Layer the cake with the vanilla cream cheese filling, then crumb-coat and mask it with the meringue buttercream following the instructions on page 172. (Reserve a little buttercream to use to stick the ghosts and meringue kisses on the cake later.) Chill until set.

Decorate the cake as close to serving it as possible to minimise the exposure to humidity. You will need a pedestal for the cake to sit on with a base that is smaller than the width of the cake. This is so that your hands can reach underneath the cake when draping the cobweb around it. This could be a small bowl turned upside down with a non-slip mat or damp cloth on top for the cake to sit on. Place the cake carefully on top of the pedestal.

Put the marshmallows in a microwaveable bowl and warm in the microwave for 10 seconds at a time until melted.

Put on some rubber gloves. Pick up a handful of the melted marshmallows and stretch it between your hands until it looks stringy then wrap it over the top and around the sides of the cake.

Repeat all over the cake until it is covered in cobwebs. The melted marshmallows can set quickly, so you may need to reheat them from time to time to soften them again.

Arrange the meringue kisses and sugar ghosts on top and around the side of the cake using dabs of buttercream to stick them on. Support the large ghost with a large meringue kiss at the back, leaning it against it so that it doesn't fall over.

Add the mini marshmallows and sprinkles on top and around the sides with the help of tweezers if you find it too tricky by hand.

Serve as soon as possible.

PERFECT LIGHTING & SCENT

When it comes to styling in your home, whether it's for yourself, your family or your guests, lighting is always key. If your space is dappled in natural sunlight, that's ideal for 'setting the stage', and during the darker months, candles and twinkling light garlands create a distinct touch of magic.

For evoking the senses and setting the mood, I am a perpetual fan of scented candles. My favourite is called White Rose & Lemon Leaves by Jo Loves, whose shop is opposite the Belgravia Parlour. We once designed a cupcake tasting experience based on this particular scent and I've been hooked on Jo's creations ever since. It's so important that the scent matches the season and I strongly feel it's worth investing what you can in good-quality candles made with natural ingredients.

Winter & Christmas

I always think it's remarkable how much inspiration used in modern culture comes from fairy tales. For us, it's especially at Christmas, when the Parlours look as though they could have jumped straight out of The Nutcracker. It feels, quite literally, like the land of cakes and sweets. Regardless of our theme, the atmosphere is of a winter wonderland that's bursting with sparkle and magic. We give a huge amount of time and attention to our festive decorations, and this is where our cakes and cookies really shine. The sense of sharing and giving, indulging and spending good times is the prerequisite to it all, and it's this spirit that feels utterly infectious.

Creativity reigns at this time of year and my team and I become very crafty — whether that's through the bakes and gifts on offer, such as our exquisite Gingerbread Cabins, or the Parlours' installation decorations. The art of producing a collection and mirroring the narrative throughout our displays always feels, to me, as though we are telling little stories. One of our most moving themes was the 2019 Sugar & Ice collection. Our range drew inspiration from the Arctic and, whilst beautiful to look at, we also took the opportunity to raise awareness about the threats to sea ice and polar bears, donating a percentage of our profits to charity.

Snowman Cookies

These adorable pink-cheeked snowman cookies never fail to give me a warm and cosy feeling. A simple vanilla cookie recipe is followed by more technical instructions on how to decorate with white sugar paste and a face, scarf and hat design, using a silicone sugar mould to achieve the cable knit effect.

MAKES 10 COOKIES

For the vanilla cookie dough

1 quantity Basic Sugar Cookie Dough (see page 165) flavoured with 1 tsp vanilla extract
plain (all-purpose) flour, for dusting

For the decoration

1 quantity Half & Half Paste (see page 166)
icing (confectioner's) sugar and cornflour (cornstarch), for dusting
a small amount of white vegetable fat (eg Trex)
pink and peppermint green food colouring pastes

black edible food pen (see Stockists, page 182)
edible blush pink blossom tint (see Stockists, page 182)
pearl edible lustre spray (see Stockists, page 182)
2 tbsp Royal Icing, soft peak consistency (see page 167), plus extra if needed

Specialist equipment (see page 164 for a basic equipment list and page 182 for stockists)

XXL snowman cookie cutter
cable silicone mould
rustic cable knit mould

TO MAKE THE COOKIES

Preheat the oven to 175°C fan/375°F/Gas 5 and line 2 baking trays with baking parchment.

Unwrap the chilled cookie dough and briefly knead it through to soften it slightly.

Place the dough onto a lightly floured work surface and roll it out to an even thickness of about 5mm (¼in).

Using the snowman cutter, stamp out 10 cookies and place them onto the lined baking trays, spaced apart by at least 1cm (½in). Ensure that there are no wrinkles in the paper under the cookies and weigh the edges of the paper down if using a fan-assisted oven, otherwise the cookies may lift up during the baking process and turn out uneven. Put the trays of cookies in the fridge to chill for about 10 minutes.

Bake in the preheated oven for 8–12 minutes, turning the trays once during baking to ensure they bake evenly. When cooked, they should look golden brown and spring back when pressing down with your finger. Allow the cookies to cool on the trays.

TO DECORATE THE COOKIES

Lightly dust a smooth surface or plastic board with cornflour and place the white half & half paste on top. Apply a thin layer of vegetable fat to a rolling pin and roll the paste out to a thickness of 1mm (1⁄32in).

Using the snowman cutter, stamp out 10 pieces. Leave them to rest on a smooth surface that has been lightly dusted with icing sugar and cornflour and cover loosely with cling film until needed.

Reserve about 50g (1¾oz) of white paste and wrap it in cling film for making the pom poms later.

Divide the remaining white paste roughly in 2 (you will need a little bit more for the pink colour) and mix the slightly larger half with pink food colouring to a light pink. Mix the other half to a light green with the

peppermint green food colouring. Wrap each paste colour individually in cling film and rest for 10 minutes to firm up.

Roll the peppermint green paste out to a thickness of about 2mm (¹⁄₁₆in) and press the cable silicone mould on top to emboss it with a wool effect pattern. Cut out 5 woolly hat shapes using the hat part of the cookie cutter. Use a small kitchen knife to trim the bottom of the hat off and press the paste against the metal sections of the hat part to emboss the lines.

Repeat for the 5 scarf pieces using the scarf section of the snowman cutter. Place the knitwear items on a smooth surface that has been lightly dusted with icing sugar or cornflour and cover with cling film until needed.

Repeat the previous 2 steps with the pink paste to make 5 pink woolly hats and scarves.

To make the pom poms for the woolly hat, roll the remaining white paste into a sausage and cut it into 10 even pieces. Roll each piece into a smooth ball. Rub the pom pom part of the cable knit mould with a thin layer of vegetable fat and press a ball inside. Trim off any excess paste and flatten the back of the pom pom, then unmould. Repeat to make 10 pom poms, greasing the mould again after each use.

Make 5 pale pink hearts using some of the leftover pale pink paste. Repeat the previous step, this time pressing each ball of the paste into the small heart shape in the cable knit mould to make 10 hearts.

Add a little bit more pink food colouring to the leftover pale pink paste and mix to a bright pink. Repeat the previous step to make another 5 hearts.

Roll the remaining bright pink paste into a sausage, cut into 10 lentil-sized pieces and shape each into a carrot-shaped nose. Cover all items with cling film until needed.

Remove the cling film from the snowman shapes – they should be semi-set and feel dry on top. Draw the eyelids and lashes onto the faces using the black edible food pen.

Spray the snowmen with the pearl edible lustre. Mix the royal icing with 1 tsp water to make a sugar glue. Brush the cookies thinly with the glue and stick the white snowman sugar shapes on top. Lightly press the paste onto the cookie while it is still slightly pliable to ensure there are no gaps between the cookie and the paste.

Add the woolly hats and scarves followed by the noses, hearts and pom poms. If the sugar glue is not strong enough to hold the smaller items, you can also stick them on using a piping bag filled with white royal icing. Let the cookies dry completely.

Add blush pink cheeks using a fine artist's brush and the blush pink blossom tint. Dip the brush in the dust colour and dab it off on a paper towel before applying the colour to the snowman.

If you're not eating them right away, store the cookies in a dry, cool place. They have a shelf life of up to 6 weeks if kept in an airtight container or wrapped in cellophane.

Cinnamon Stars

These cookies are a modern twist on a German Christmas classic, which always takes me straight back to childhood. Vanilla- and cinnamon-spiced hazelnut and almond stars are topped with pearlised meringue icing in shades of pink, white and ice blue. The trick is using the correct cutter. A specialist cinnamon star cutter which opens up to release the cookie is recommended for perfect results and can be found online.

MAKES ABOUT 60 STARS

For the cinnamon dough

3 egg whites
225g (8oz/1⅔ cups) icing (confectioner's) sugar, sifted (plus extra for dusting)
150g (5½oz/1½ cups) ground almonds
225g (8oz/2¼cups) ground hazelnuts
1½ tbsp ground cinnamon
pinch of salt
finely grated zest of 2 oranges
290g (10¼oz) marzipan, diced into small pieces

For the meringue topping

6 egg whites
450g (1lb/3¼ cups) icing (confectioner's) sugar, sifted
pink and blue food colouring pastes
pearl edible lustre spray (see Stockists, page 182)

Specialist equipment (see page 164 for a basic equipment list and page 182 for stockists)

stepped palette knife
foldable cinnamon star cutter

TO MAKE THE CINNAMON DOUGH

Put the egg whites into the mixing bowl of an electric mixer fitted with a whisk attachment and whisk to a soft peak consistency.

While whisking on a medium speed, gradually add the icing sugar and keep whisking until stiff and glossy.

Mix together the ground almonds, ground hazelnuts, cinnamon, salt and orange zest in a bowl. Add this mixture to the meringue and mix everything together on a low speed using a paddle attachment.

Slowly add the marzipan, while still mixing, until the mixture comes together to form a sticky dough.

Line a baking tray with a sheet of baking parchment and dust it with icing sugar. Place the dough on top and flatten it with your hands as much as possible. Dust the top of the dough with icing sugar too, and place another sheet of baking parchment on top.

Roll the dough out between the 2 sheets of paper to an even thickness of about 1cm (½in).

Chill the dough in the fridge while you make the meringue topping.

TO MAKE THE MERINGUE TOPPING

Put the egg whites into the mixing bowl of an electric mixer fitted with a whisk attachment and whisk to a soft peak consistency.

While whisking, gradually add the icing sugar and keep whisking until stiff and glossy.

Divide the meringue into 4 equal quantities. Colour one portion a pastel shade of pink with a small amount of pink food colouring, one to a darker pink, another to a pastel blue with a small amount of blue food colouring and keep the final portion white. Be careful not to add too much colouring, as paste is much more concentrated than liquid. (For colouring meringue instructions, see page 180.)

TO ICE AND BAKE THE CINNAMON STARS

Preheat the oven to 110°C fan/250°F/Gas ½ and line 2 baking trays with baking parchment.

Cut the cinnamon dough into 4 equal sections. Using the stepped palette knife, spread a different coloured meringue over each section of dough in a smooth, thin layer.

Using the cinnamon star cutter, stamp out star shapes and place them onto the lined baking trays. Push the cutter halves together when stamping out the cookie, and let them come apart to release the stars onto the tray. Dip and clean the cutter after each star by dipping it into water. This will prevent the dough from sticking to the cutter and ensure the star shapes remain sharp and pointy.

Once you have cut all the stars out, scrape the meringue off the trimmings and re-roll them once. Cover them with meringue again to cut out a few more. (Note, you can only re-roll the dough once.)

Bake the cinnamon stars for 1½ hours, until they easily lift off the tray and feel firm – you don't want them to colour. Remove from the oven and allow to cool on the trays.

When cold, spray the tops lightly with the pearl edible lustre spray.

If stored in an airtight container, the cinnamon stars will last for up to 3 weeks.

Gingerbread Cabins

This adorable miniature version of a classic gingerbread house is a little feast for all the senses. A spiced gingerbread cookie is hand decorated with royal icing and sugar paste. If presented in a beautiful gift box, it makes a touching handmade gift for Christmas. Store gingerbread cookies in an airtight container and they will last for weeks.

MAKES 12 COOKIES

For the gingerbread dough

140g (5oz/¾ cup less 2 tsp) light brown sugar
5 tsp treacle
5 tsp golden syrup (light corn syrup)
3 tbsp water
2 tbsp ground ginger
2 tbsp ground cinnamon
½ tsp ground cloves
165g (5¾oz/⅔ cup plus 1 tbsp) salted butter, cold and diced
½ tsp bicarbonate of soda (baking soda), sifted
375g (13¼oz/3 cups less 2 tbsp) plain (all-purpose) flour, plus extra for dusting

For the decoration

½ quantity Royal Icing (see page 167)
400g (14oz) Half & Half paste (made with 200g/7oz of sugar paste and 200g/7oz of sugar florist paste, see page 166)

claret pink, peppermint green and chestnut brown food colouring pastes (see Stockists, page 182)
icing (confectioner's) sugar and cornflour (cornstarch), for dusting
a small amount of white vegetable fat (eg Trex)
caster sugar, for sprinkling
black edible food pen (see Stockists, page 182)

Specialist equipment (see page 164 for a basic equipment list and page 182 for stockists)

gingerbread house cutter set
10cm (4in) and 4cm (1½in) round fluted cookie cutters
9cm (3½ in) round cookie cutter
1–2cm (½–¾in) small heart cutter
6cm (2½in) deer/fawn cookie cutter
6cm (2½in) small Christmas tree cookie cutter
2 small piping bags, or make 2 of your own paper piping bags (see page 168)

TO MAKE THE GINGERBREAD COOKIES

Put the sugar, treacle, golden syrup, water, ground ginger, cinnamon and cloves into a deep saucepan and bring to the boil while stirring constantly. Remove from the heat and gradually add the diced butter. Stir until combined.

Add the bicarbonate of soda while whisking constantly – take care as the mixture will bubble up. Transfer into the bowl of an electric mixer, cover with a towel or cling film and leave to cool down to room temperature.

Sift the flour into the batter and slowly mix together to a slightly wet and sticky dough using a paddle attachment. Wrap the dough in cling film and chill for 2 hours or until cool and firm.

While the dough is chilling, line 2 baking trays with baking parchment.

Remove the dough from the fridge and gently knead it and form into a smooth ball.

Place the dough onto a work surface lightly dusted with flour and roll it out to a thickness of 5mm (¼in).

Using the gingerbread house cutter, stamp out 12 cabin cookies and place them on the prepared baking trays.

Chill the cookies again for 30 minutes. Meanwhile, preheat the oven to 180°C fan/400°F/Gas 6.

Bake the cookies for 8–10 minutes until they spring back to the touch and the edges are slightly darkened. Leave to cool on the trays.

TO DECORATE THE COOKIES

Following the instructions for colouring half & half paste on page 166, use claret pink food colouring to colour half of the half & half paste to a pastel pink.

Lightly dust a smooth surface or plastic board with cornflour and place the pastel pink paste on top. Apply a thin layer of vegetable fat to a rolling pin and roll the paste out to a thickness of 1mm (⅟₃₂in).

Using the door cookie cutter from the gingerbread house cutter set, stamp out 12 door shapes. Wrap any remaining pink paste in cling film to reserve for later use.

Mix 1 tbsp white royal icing with 1 tsp water to make a sugar glue. Brush a thin layer of the glue onto the cookies where the door will go and stick the doors on top.

Roll the white paste out to 1mm (⅟₃₂in) thickness and stamp out 12 fluted circles using the large round fluted cutter.

Cut the inner part of the fluted circles out with the plain round cutter, so that you end up with a hoop with a thin fluted border. Cut the border at one point to open it up.

Brush a thin line of sugar glue around the pink doors and arrange the fluted borders around them. Trim the bottoms neatly so that they sit flush with the base line of the door.

Add a little bit more food colouring to the reserved pale pink paste and mix it to a darker shade of pink.

Roll the dark pink paste out to 1mm (⅟₃₂in) thickness and cut out 12 small fluted circles. Then stamp heart shaped windows out of the centres using the small heart cutter.

Using the sugar glue, stick the windows on the cookies, positioning them above the doors.

Divide the remaining white paste into 2 portions. Colour one half of the paste a pale peppermint green shade and the other a pale chestnut brown shade using the relevant food colouring pastes. Wrap the brown paste in cling film and let it rest until later use.

Roll the green paste out to 1mm (⅟₃₂in) thickness and use the tree cookie cutter to stamp out 12 tree shapes. Using the sugar glue, stick one onto the right-hand side of each door, slightly overlapping it.

Roll out the pale brown paste to 1mm (⅟₃₂in) thickness and cut out 12 fawn shapes with the fawn cookie cutter. The legs are very narrow and the paste might get stuck in the cutter. If this happens, lightly grease the cutter with vegetable fat before each use and the paste should come out more easily. You can also use a fine artist's brush or thin sugar modelling tool to push the legs out carefully. Let the fawns semi set on a smooth surface lightly dusted with icing sugar or cornflour before sticking them onto the cookies to prevent the legs from stretching.

Mix about 3 tbsp royal icing with a few drops of water to achieve a soft peak piping consistency (see page 167 for more guidance on royal icing consistencies).

Spoon the icing into a small piping bag and snip a tiny tip off the end. Pipe the delicate details on the fawn. Then pipe the dots around the edge of the pink window frame.

Cut the hole of the piping bag a little larger and pipe the snow on the trees. Start by piping a row of small-pearl-sized dots along the bottom branch of the trees. Dampen a soft, fine artist's brush with water and using the 'brush embroidery technique', push the brush down the middle of each dot and drag the icing upward to a point. Clean your brush after each use and dampen it with water from time to time. Ensure the brush is damp and not wet as the water can melt the icing. Repeat for the upper layers of the trees.

Mix about 4 tbsp royal icing with some water to make it a runny 'flooding' consistency. Fill a piping bag with it and keep the remainder in a bowl covered with a damp cloth until you need more.

Using the piping bag filled with the soft peak royal icing, pipe the outline for the snow-covered rooftop and chimney, including the icicles.

Flood the centres of the snow-covered roofs using the piping bag containing the runny royal icing.

While the icing is still wet, sprinkle caster sugar over the top for a snowy texture.

Repeat for all the cookies and let them dry completely.

To finish, draw the eye lids on the fawns' faces using the black edible food pen.

Once dry, store the cookies in a dry, cool place. Gingerbread cookies have a shelf life of up to 8 weeks if kept in an airtight container or wrapped in cellophane.

Cable Knit

COCONUT & ALMOND CAKE

Exquisitely dressed for the festive season, this beautiful cake is cleverly decorated with a cosy cable knit effect, and each slice is topped with a pearlised chocolate crunch ball, a pretty sugar snowflake and metallic sugar pearls. Inside is a lovely and light almond-infused chiffon sponge layered with a smooth coconut meringue buttercream. The piping effect may look challenging, but once you're in the flow it's surprisingly quick to get the hang of. I suggest practising for a bit before piping directly onto the cake.

MAKES A 15CM (6IN) CAKE (SERVES 10)

1 quantity Chiffon Sponge (3 x 15cm/6in cakes, see page 171) flavoured with 1 tsp vanilla extract

For the sugar snowflakes
50g (1¾oz) white sugar florist paste
a small amount of white vegetable fat (eg Trex)
icing (confectioner's) sugar and cornflour (cornstarch), for dusting
pearl edible lustre spray (see Stockists, page 182)

For the almond sugar syrup
100g (3½oz/½ cup) caster sugar
100ml (3½fl oz/scant ½ cup) water
natural almond extract or almond liqueur (such as Amaretto), to taste

For the coconut meringue buttercream
1 layer cake quantity Meringue Buttercream (see page 176)
170g (11¾oz/1½ cups) coconut cream (thick)

For the decoration
10 pearlescent choco balls (large) in pink, blue and ivory (see Stockists, page 182)
small silver and pink metallic sugar pearls (see Stockists, page 182)

Specialist equipment (see page 164 for a basic equipment list and page 182 for stockists)
mini snowflake plunger cutter
3 x 15cm (6in) shallow cake tins
fine-toothed side scraper
large piping bag fitted with a small star nozzle

TO MAKE THE SUGAR SNOWFLAKES

Mix the sugar florist paste with a small amount of vegetable fat to a smooth pliable paste.

Lightly dust a smooth surface or plastic board with cornflour and place the sugar florist paste on top. Apply a thin layer of vegetable fat to a small rolling pin and roll the paste out to a thickness of 1mm (1⁄32in).

Using the mini snowflake plunger cutter, stamp out 10 pieces (plus a few extra in case of breakages).

Leave the snowflakes to rest on a smooth surface that has been lightly dusted with icing sugar or cornflour and spray the tops with pearl edible lustre. Let them dry completely – this will take a few hours or you can make them well in advance.

TO MAKE THE ALMOND SUGAR SYRUP

Put the sugar and water in a saucepan, bring to a boil and cook until the sugar is dissolved. Remove from the heat and allow to cool.

Once cool, add the almond extract or liqueur.

TO MAKE THE COCONUT MERINGUE BUTTERCREAM

Once you have made the meringue buttercream, fold in the coconut cream and mix until combined.

TO ASSEMBLE AND DECORATE THE CAKE

Layer and crumb coat the baked chiffon sponge layers using the coconut meringue buttercream and the almond syrup, as per the instructions on page 172. Chill for 30 minutes or until set.

Once the crumb coat has set, mask the cake with another layer of buttercream to cover any crumb that may still be exposed. While the masking coat is still soft, scrape around the sides with the fine-toothed side scraper in one swoop to achieve a narrow lined effect.

Tidy up the cake top with the palette knife by spreading the overlapping buttercream from the top edge toward the middle of the cake and let the buttercream set in the fridge for a few minutes.

Spoon the remaining buttercream into a large piping bag fitted with a small star nozzle.

Divide the side of the cake into 10 even sections and mark them with a knife along the top edge of the cake.

Starting at one of the marks, pipe a vertical line of scallop shells from the top of the cake all the way down to the bottom. Repeat for all 10 sections of the cake.

Now pipe a vertical row of interlocking S-shaped scrolls, starting at the top edge and running all the way down to the bottom of the cake, and centred between 2 rows of the scallop shells.

Pipe 10 evenly-sized and -spaced out rosettes of buttercream around the top of the cake and top them with alternating colours of large choco balls.

Add the sugar snowflakes between the rosettes and a sprinkle of metallic sugar pearls for a festive effect.

THE MAGIC OF A CREATIVE TEAM

At this point, I must give acclaim to my full creative 'dream team'. With every collection at the Parlours, we work tirelessly to join up all the dots. I have built long-standing relationships with like-minded experts who have helped to grow and define my style by adding their talent, vision and expertise to each incubated idea. From my development chefs, to my photographer, florist, copywriter and graphic designer, it requires such precision to translate and deliver my message to the outside world — allowing it to unfold in layers across the cake art, the floral features, the graphics, imagery and language. It's this that captivates our audience, bringing joy to those who feel a connection with our offering.

This creative energy can be recreated on a smaller level at home. From finding brands that inspire you not only in design but also in making eco-conscious choices, to following inspirational individuals on social media, this all helps to define your style ambition. Online tutorials and workshops add to your story and allow you to evolve your at-home displays and also give you memories and stories to run alongside.

When it comes to styling at the Parlours, my florist and stylist Mathew Dickinson is our luminary. Our relationship goes way back to my time in the wedding industry. Mathew and I instantly clicked and have been a creative team ever since the Parlour's first floral display in 2015. He has remarkable vision and pushes creative boundaries that may sound overly abstract on paper. However, I trust him implicitly and this 'free rein' is what allows us to create magic with each installation. Whether or not you have a creative partner in crime, Mathew's top tips below are well worth keeping in mind for any styling conundrum:

* Always keep it simple.
* Set a theme and stick to it — don't get sidetracked.
* Select a well-defined colour palette, make sure your choices tone well together and keep to it. Too many colours will give a confused result.
* Be unique. Social media platforms and especially Pinterest are very useful for generating ideas, but your style needs to feel authentic to you.
* Visualising what will photograph well, as well as sketching and making collages, all help to clarify what you are trying to achieve.
* Avoid over-cluttering. It's easy to do, but generally speaking, less is always more.
* It won't always be perfect, but you learn from your mistakes more than anything else.
* Stay positive about what you do at all times!

Winter Village

GINGERBREAD & SPECULOOS CAKE

A festive Christmas centrepiece, and an opportunity to share your very own masterpiece baked with love. Inspired by the spiced cookie that's so popular especially in Germany, Belgium and the Netherlands, this recipe combines a scrumptious speculoos sponge, layered with yummy caramelised cookie spread and masked with speculoos meringue buttercream. The hand-piped winter village cake toppers are made of gingerbread cookies and will fill your room with warming aromas of sugar and spice.

MAKES A 15CM (6IN) CAKE (SERVES 10)

For the gingerbread cookies

105g (3½oz/½ cup) light brown sugar
1½ tbsp treacle
1½ tbsp golden syrup (light corn syrup)
1½ tbsp ground ginger
1½ tbsp ground cinnamon
½ tsp ground cloves
2½ tbsp water
125g (4½oz/½ cup plus 1 tbsp) salted butter, cold and diced
½ tsp bicarbonate of soda (baking soda), sifted
280g (10oz/2 cups plus 2 tbsp) plain (all-purpose) flour, (plus extra for dusting)
2 heaped tbsp Royal Icing (see page 167)
1 tbsp caster sugar

For the vanilla sugar syrup

75g (2½oz/⅓ cup) caster sugar
75ml (2½fl oz/⅓ cup) water
½ tsp vanilla extract

For the caramel sponge

90g (3¼oz/6 tbsp) unsalted butter
pinch of salt
200g (7oz/1 cup) caster sugar
120g (4¼oz/⅔ cup less 1 tbsp) dark brown sugar
1 tsp vanilla extract
3 medium eggs
225g (8oz/1¾ cups) plain (all-purpose) flour
190g (6¾oz/¾ cup) buttermilk
1 tsp white wine vinegar
½ tsp bicarbonate of soda (baking soda)

For the speculoos filling

about 150g (5½oz) crunchy speculoos spread (eg Lotus Biscoff)

For the speculoos meringue buttercream

35ml (2 tbsp) water
150g (5½oz/¾ cup) caster sugar
80g (2¾oz) egg whites (from approx. 3 eggs)
200g (7oz/¾ cup plus 2 tbsp) unsalted butter, diced and softened
175g (6oz/⅔ cup) smooth speculoos spread (eg Lotus Biscoff)

For the decorations

star aniseed
a few white mini meringue kisses (store-bought: see Stockists, page 182 – or make your own: see Meringue Kisses, page 180)
white mini sugar pearls

Specialist equipment (see page 164 for a basic equipment list and page 182 for stockists)

cocktail sticks (toothpicks)
selection of mini gingerbread house cookie cutters
selection of mini Christmas tree cookie cutters
2 small piping bags, or make 2 of your own paper piping bags (see page 168)
3 x 15cm (6in) shallow cake tins
15cm (6in) thin cake board
piping bag

TO MAKE AND DECORATE THE GINGERBREAD COOKIES

Soak about 10 cocktail sticks in water.

Put the sugar, treacle, golden syrup, ground ginger, cinnamon and cloves and water into a deep saucepan and bring to the boil while stirring constantly. Remove from the heat and gradually add the diced butter. Stir until combined.

Add the bicarbonate of soda while whisking constantly – take care as the mixture will swell up. Transfer into the bowl of an electric mixer, cover with a towel or cling film and leave to cool down to room temperature.

Sift the flour on top of the batter and slowly mix together to a slightly wet and sticky dough using a paddle attachment. Wrap the dough in cling film and chill for 2 hours or until cool and firm.

While the dough is chilling, line a baking tray with baking parchment.

Remove the dough from the fridge and gently knead it and form into a smooth ball.

Place the dough onto a smooth surface lightly dusted with flour and roll it out to a thickness of 3–4mm (⅛in).

Cut out 3 different-sized gingerbread houses, and a few Christmas trees and place them on the prepared tray. (Any leftover dough can be frozen for up to 1 month or used to make more cookies for the Christmas table. A selection of mini gingerbread men always goes down a treat if served with mulled wine or hot chocolate during the festive season.)

Push a few soaked cocktail sticks halfway into the bottom of each cookie; these will later be pushed into the cake to help the cookies stand upright.

Chill the cookies again for 20 minutes. Meanwhile, preheat the oven to 180°C fan/400°F/Gas 6.

Bake the cookies for 6–8 minutes until they spring back to the touch and the edges are slightly darkened. Leave to cool on the tray.

Mix 1 tbsp royal icing with a drop of water to achieve a soft peak piping consistency (see page 167 for guidance on royal icing consistencies).

Spoon the icing into a small piping bag and snip a small tip off the end. Pipe the outlines for the snow along the rooftops, chimneys and windowsills on the houses.

Pipe squiggly lines across the trees and sprinkle with some of the caster sugar while the icing is wet to give the icing a snowy texture.

Mix the remaining royal icing with a little bit more water to a runny consistency and spoon it into another small piping bag. Snip a small tip off the end and use this runny icing to flood the middles of the outlines on the houses.

While the icing is still wet, sprinkle the caster sugar over the top and allow to dry.

TO MAKE THE VANILLA SUGAR SYRUP

Put the sugar, water and vanilla extract in a saucepan, bring to a boil and cook until the sugar is dissolved. Remove from the heat and allow to cool.

TO MAKE THE CARAMEL SPONGES

Preheat the oven to 175°C fan/375°F/Gas 5. Grease 3 x 15cm (6in) shallow cake tins with oil spray and line the bases with baking parchment.

Put the butter, salt, both sugars and vanilla extract into the bowl of an electric mixer fitted with a paddle attachment and beat at medium–high speed until pale and fluffy. This will take a while, so do this as a first step to allow plenty of time to aerate the mixture.

Lightly beat the eggs in a separate bowl, then slowly pour them into the butter and sugar mix while beating on medium speed. Watch as the eggs combine with the butter mix and stop pouring if the batter needs time to come together, then add more. The eggs and butter should both be at room temperature to avoid splitting. However, should the mixture split, add 1 tbsp flour to bring the batter back together before adding more egg.

Alternating between the 2, add the flour and the buttermilk to the batter in batches and mix until combined.

Mix the vinegar and bicarbonate of soda together in a small bowl and immediately, as it bubbles up, add it to the batter.

Divide the batter evenly between the 3 prepared cake tins.

Bake in the preheated oven for 30–35 minutes, depending on your oven. The sponges are cooked when the edges come away from the sides of the cake tin and the tops spring back to the touch. A skewer inserted in the middle of the sponge should come out clean when ready.

Leave the sponges to rest in the tins for a few minutes and brush the tops with the sugar syrup. This will prevent the cakes from forming a hard crust and the heat will ensure the moisture and flavour are absorbed evenly.

Once slightly cooled, unmould the sponges from the cake tins carefully without breaking the edges – use a small kitchen knife to release the sides if required. Leave to cool completely on a wire rack.

TO MAKE THE SPECULOOS MERINGUE BUTTERCREAM

Make the meringue buttercream following the instructions on page 176, but using the quantities listed in this recipe on page 148.

Once you have made the meringue buttercream, fold in the smooth speculoos spread and mix until combined.

TO ASSEMBLE AND DECORATE THE CAKE

Start following the instructions for preparing the cake on page 172, up to the stage at which you've placed the first sponge layer on the cake board.

Spoon 2 tbsp of the speculoos buttercream into a piping bag and snip a medium tip off the end. Pipe a 5mm (¼in) thick ring around the edge of the

sponge layer. Use a spoon to fill the buttercream ring with the crunchy speculoos spread.

Place the middle sponge layer on top (the one that has been trimmed on both sides).

Using a palette knife, spread an even layer of speculoos buttercream on top of the sponge, about 5mm (¼in) thick.

Place the third sponge on top, brown side up.

Ensure that all the sponges are centred and the top of the cake is level. Tidy up any bits of buttercream that are squeezing out from around the edges with a palette knife.

Coat the cake all around with more buttercream using a palette knife and side scraper. The first buttercream coat is also called a 'crumb coat' as its purpose is to hold the crumbs in place and create a solid basic shape. It doesn't have to be perfect and it's fine if some cake crumb shows through the buttercream. Let the buttercream set in the fridge for another 30 minutes.

Once the crumb coat has set, mask the cake with a perfectly smooth and even layer of buttercream.

Create a swirl on the top using the palette knife and turntable. Hold the tip of the palette knife down into buttercream, starting in the centre of the cake top. Start swivelling the turntable and, as it spins, gradually move the palette knife toward the outside until you reach the edge. Transfer the cake back to the fridge and chill until the buttercream has set.

Stick the gingerbread cookies into the cake top, arranging them in a village formation, with the larger cookies at the back.

Place the star aniseeds and meringue kisses around the village and sprinkle white sugar pearls over the top for some snow.

WARNING

Ensure that all the cocktail sticks are removed from the cake and cookies before eating and do not let them get into the hands of little people!

WINTER & CHRISTMAS STYLE SECRETS

There's something profoundly comforting about arriving home for Christmas and being greeted with the scent of sugar and spice. Our Parlours are filled with this aroma from early November, and it's something that can easily be replicated at home, even without a team of pastry chefs. With this in mind, you can quite literally deck the halls and create edible hanging ornaments with decorated gingerbread cookies. If you can keep them away from any humidity, the gingerbread will last for weeks. It's a wonderful activity to involve the children in and the gingerbread can even be used as place settings and edible gifts.

Follow my Gingerbread Cookie recipe (page 140) and once decorated, my top tip is to let the icing dry completely overnight. You'll need a fine drill for the next part (and this is for adults only), but don't be put off, as the results are well worth it. A 4–5mm (¼in) diameter drill attachment is ideal; do ensure you clean and sanitise it before use. Place the cookies on a wire rack and drill holes for the ribbons to go through. I've tried different techniques over the years and this is the fastest and cleanest way to hang your gingerbread characters. To go a step further, a gingerbread house on a mantelpiece or my Winter Village Gingerbread and Speculoos Cake (page 148) on your Christmas table make stunning centrepieces.

If, like me, you're always drawn to pastel colours, don't be afraid to embrace this theme at Christmas. There are so many beautiful decorations to suit this look and it stands apart from the more traditional displays of reds and greens. Beyond your Christmas tree, you can have great fun draping snowy garlands of faux pine around windows, doors and fireplaces, adding extra decoration with pastel baubles, fairy lights and your gingerbread cookies.

Christmas in Germany centres around the sharing of food, and I always love the idea of creating a 'land of sweets'-inspired theme at home, keeping visitors well fed with glass jars of confectionery, candy canes and iced cookies. One of my favourite decorations is a more abstract 'candy Christmas tree'. I created a Parlour full of them, adorning our shelves, a few years ago and they made such an impact. You can purchase papier mâché or polystyrene cones online, and the trick is to cover them with royal icing, which then allows you to stick cinnamon stars, meringue kisses and macarons all over. If you have a gingerbread house, the cones create a wonderful effect when placed either side on a mantelpiece.

Arctic Ice

PEPPERMINT & CHOCOLATE CHIP CUPCAKES

This is a wonderful recipe to awaken your inner child with the nostalgic flavour of peppermint frosting. When combined with the delightfully light and fluffy chocolate chip sponge the result is entirely rewarding. Follow my step-by-step instructions to create your own sugar polar bears and snowflakes to decorate these frosty-themed cupcakes.

MAKES 24 CUPCAKES

For the sugar decorations
250g (9oz) sugar florist paste
a small amount of white vegetable fat (eg Trex)
icing (confectioner's) sugar or cornflour (cornstarch),
  for dusting
black edible food pen (see Stockists, page 182)
edible blush pink blossom tint (see Stockists, page 182)
pearl edible lustre spray (see Stockists, page 182)
pink and silver metallic sugar balls

For the meringue icebergs
6 egg whites
450g (1lb/3¼ cups) icing (confectioner's) sugar, sifted
pearl edible lustre spray

For the peppermint sugar syrup
150g (5½oz/¾ cup) caster sugar
150ml (5fl oz/scant ⅔ cup) water
peppermint extract, to taste (see Stockists, page 182)

For the chocolate chip cupcakes
225g (8oz/1 cup) unsalted butter, softened
pinch of salt
225g (8oz/1 cup plus 2 tbsp) caster sugar
1 tsp vanilla extract
4 eggs, at room temperature
225g (8oz/1¾ cups) self-raising flour, sifted
80g (2¾oz) dark chocolate chips (53% cocoa solids),
  roughly chopped

For the peppermint meringue buttercream
1 cupcake quantity Meringue Buttercream (see
  page 176)
5 drops of peppermint extract
ice blue food colouring paste (see Stockists, page 182)

**Specialist equipment (see page 164 for a basic
  equipment list and page 182 for stockists)**
mini polar bear cutter
mini snowflake plunger cutter
stepped palette knife
2 x 12-hole cupcake baking trays
24 silver metallic baking cases
large piping bag
large piping bag fitted with a large star nozzle

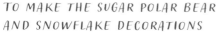

TO MAKE THE SUGAR POLAR BEAR AND SNOWFLAKE DECORATIONS

Mix the sugar florist paste with a small amount of vegetable fat to a smooth, pliable paste. Remove any dry and brittle pieces of paste before kneading it, as it will spoil the batch and look lumpy.

Lightly dust a smooth surface or plastic board with cornflour and place the sugar florist paste on top. Apply a thin layer of vegetable fat to a small rolling pin and roll the paste out to a thickness of 1mm (1/32in).

Using the polar bear cookie cutter, stamp out 24 bears (plus a few extra in case of breakages). Leave them to dry on a smooth surface that has been lightly dusted with icing sugar or cornflour.

Roll out some more paste and stamp out about 48 snowflakes (plus a few spare) using the plunger cutter. Ensure that you press the plunger cutter down firmly to emboss the snowflake pattern on the paste before lifting it off. Leave the snowflakes to dry with the polar bears.

Once dry, draw the eyelids and noses onto the polar bear faces using the black edible food pen.

Dip a fine artist's brush into the blush pink blossom tint, dab the dust off slightly on a paper towel and apply the pink petal dust to the bears' bellies.

Spray the snowflakes and polar bears with the pearl lustre spray.

TO MAKE THE MERINGUE ICEBERGS

Preheat the oven to 80°C fan/210°F/Gas ¼. Line a baking tray with baking parchment or a silpat mat.

Put the egg whites into the bowl of an electric mixer fitted with a whisk attachment and whisk to soft peaks.

Gradually add the icing sugar, while whisking, and keep whisking until the meringue is stiff and glossy.

Thinly spread the meringue over the prepared tray using the stepped palette knife.

Bake in the preheated oven for about 30 minutes, until the meringue feels firm and lifts off the tray. Allow the meringue to cool on the tray.

Spray the meringue with pearl edible lustre spray, then break it into small triangular shards that resemble the shape of icebergs. Store in an airtight container or cover with cling film if not using right away.

TO MAKE THE PEPPERMINT SUGAR SYRUP

Put the sugar and water in a saucepan, bring to a boil and cook until the sugar is dissolved. Remove from the heat and allow to cool.

Once cool, add the peppermint extract.

TO MAKE THE CHOCOLATE CHIP CUPCAKES

Preheat the oven to 175°C fan/375°F/Gas 5 and line the cupcake trays with the baking cases.

Put the butter, salt, sugar and vanilla extract into the bowl of an electric mixer fitted with a paddle attachment and cream together until pale and fluffy.

Beat the eggs in a separate bowl, and slowly add to the butter and sugar mixture, making sure they are fully incorporated and the mixture hasn't split.

Fold in the flour in 3 batches, then mix in the chocolate chips.

Fill a large piping bag with the batter and snip 2.5cm (1in) off the tip. Pipe the batter into the baking cases, filling each one about two-thirds full. Start in the centre of the base of the case, then move the piping bag up and around the outside of the case, leaving a dip in the middle; this will ensure that the cupcakes rise more evenly.

Tap the tray down a couple of times on the work surface and leave to rest for 10 minutes before baking them (I find that this prevents the cupcakes from rising too high and cracking open at the top during the baking process).

Bake in the preheated oven for 12–15 minutes. The cupcakes are cooked when they are golden, the tops spring back to the touch and the edges of the baking cases have shrunk away from the sides of the baking tray.

Remove from the oven and leave to rest in the cupcake trays for a few minutes.

Brush the tops of the cakes with the peppermint sugar syrup while still hot. This will ensure the sponges absorb the moisture and prevent a dry crust from forming.

Transfer the cupcakes to a wire rack and leave to cool completely. Wipe the bottoms with a damp cloth if sticky from the syrup. Do not leave the cupcakes to cool in the cupcake tray, as the cases may stick to the tray.

TO MAKE THE PEPPERMINT MERINGUE BUTTERCREAM

Once you have made the meringue buttercream, add the peppermint extract to taste and mix until well combined.

Mix about 1 tbsp of the buttercream with a small amount of ice blue food colouring and blend together with a palette knife until all the colour specks have dispersed. Add the coloured buttercream back into the white batch, a little at a time, and mix until you get an even pastel ice blue colour.

TO DECORATE THE CUPCAKES

Spoon the buttercream into a large piping bag fitted with a large star nozzle and pipe a large rosette on top of each cupcake.

Arrange 2 meringue icebergs on top, one polar bear and 2 snowflakes. Sprinkle with pink metallic sugar balls to finish.

Once decorated, serve as soon as possible. The sugar decorations will melt if exposed to humid conditions (such as in a refrigerator) and will only last for up to one day once placed on the cupcakes.

Baileys & Chocolate Cake

A festive Christmas indulgence just for the grown-ups. Caramel buttermilk sponge is soaked with Baileys syrup and layered with sumptuous chocolate and Baileys cream cheese filling. Artfully decorated in a stripy pink and Baileys-brown buttercream design, this cake is a winner for any sophisticated feast.

MAKES A 15CM (6IN) CAKE (SERVES 10)

For the Baileys and chocolate filling

50ml (1¾fl oz/3½ tbsp) Baileys liqueur
½ tsp liquid glucose
75g (2½oz) dark chocolate chips (53% cocoa solids)
40g (1½oz/3 tbsp) unsalted butter, softened
75g (2½oz/½ cup plus ½ tbsp) icing (confectioner's) sugar, sifted
35g (1¼oz/2½ tbsp) full-fat cream cheese, preferably Philadelphia

For the Baileys sugar syrup

100g (3½oz/½ cup) caster sugar
100ml (3½fl oz/scant ½ cup) water
50ml (1¾fl oz/3½ tbsp) Baileys liqueur

For the caramel buttermilk sponge

90g (3¼oz/6 tbsp) unsalted butter
pinch of salt
200g (7oz/1 cup) caster sugar
120g (4¼oz/½ cup plus 2 tbsp) dark brown sugar
1 tsp vanilla extract
3 medium eggs
225g (8oz/1¾ cups) plain (all-purpose) flour
190g (6¾oz/¾ cup) buttermilk
1 tsp white wine vinegar
½ tsp bicarbonate of soda (baking soda)

For the meringue buttercream

1 layer cake quantity Meringue Buttercream (see page 176)
fuchsia and dark brown food colouring pastes (see Stockists, page 182)

For the decorations

10 pink pearlescent choco balls (see Stockists, page 182)
10 small sugar snowflakes (store-bought: see Stockists, page 182 – or make your own: see Cable Knit Coconut & Almond Cake, page 145)
snowflake sprinkles (see Stockists, page 182)
pink, silver and metallic mini sugar pearls (see Stockists, page 182)

Specialist equipment (see page 164 for a basic equipment list and page 182 for stockists)

3 x 15cm (6in) shallow cake tins
15cm (6in) thin cake board
stripe contour comb
3 piping bags
piping bag fitted with a small star nozzle

TO MAKE THE BAILEYS AND CHOCOLATE FILLING

Put the Baileys and liquid glucose into a small saucepan and bring to a simmer.

Put the chocolate chips into a heatproof bowl. Add the hot Baileys to the chocolate and whisk until smooth and combined.

Cover with cling film and allow to cool down to room temperature until soft set.

Put the butter and icing sugar into the bowl of an electric mixer fitted with a paddle attachment and cream together until pale and fluffy.

In a bowl, soften the cream cheese with a spatula until smooth and add to the butter mixture. Mix until well combined.

Add the cooled but soft Baileys ganache to the cream cheese frosting in 3 additions, and mix until combined. Chill until ready to use.

TO MAKE THE BAILEYS SUGAR SYRUP

Put the sugar and water in a saucepan, bring to a boil and cook until the sugar is dissolved. Remove from the heat and allow to cool.

Once cool, add the Baileys liqueur.

TO MAKE THE CARAMEL BUTTERMILK SPONGES

Preheat the oven to 175°C fan/375°F/Gas 5. Grease 3 x 15cm (6in) shallow cake tins with oil spray and line the bases with baking parchment.

Put the butter, salt, both sugars and the vanilla extract into the bowl of an electric mixer fitted with a paddle attachment and beat at medium–high speed until pale and fluffy. This will take a while, so do this as a first step to allow plenty of time to aerate the mixture.

In another bowl, lightly beat the eggs, then slowly pour them into the butter and sugar mix while beating on medium speed. Watch as the eggs combine with the butter mix and stop pouring if the batter needs time to come together, then add more. The eggs and butter should both be at room temperature to avoid splitting. However, should the mixture split, add 1 tbsp flour to bring the batter back together before adding more egg.

Alternating between the 2, add the flour and the buttermilk to the batter in batches and mix until combined.

Mix the vinegar and bicarbonate of soda together in a small bowl and immediately, as it bubbles up, add to the batter.

Divide the batter evenly between the 3 prepared cake tins.

Bake in the preheated oven for 30–35 minutes. The sponges are cooked when the edges come away from the sides of the cake tin and the tops spring back to the touch.

Leave the sponges to rest in the tins for about 10–15 minutes.

Once slightly cooled, unmould the sponges from the cake tins carefully without breaking the edges – use a small kitchen knife to release the sides if required. Leave to cool completely on a wire rack.

TO ASSEMBLE AND DECORATE THE CAKE

If required, soften the Baileys and chocolate filling using a rubber spatula until spreadable. Start following the instructions for preparing the cake on page 172, up to the stage at which you've placed the first sponge layer on the cake board. Put 4 heaped tbsp of the meringue buttercream into a piping bag, snip a medium tip off the end. Pipe a 5mm (¼in) thick ring around the edge of the sponge layer. Use a spoon to fill the buttercream ring with the Baileys filling. Resume the instructions on page 172 to assemble, crumb coat and chill the cake, adding another ring of buttercream and Baileys filling centre between the second and third sponge layers.

Once the crumb coat has set, mask the cake with a smooth and even layer of meringue buttercream.

This time, apply a slightly thicker, smooth coat of buttercream – about 5mm (¼in) – around the sides. Go around a few times if not perfect the first time.

Using the stripe contour comb, scrape 3 deep grooves around the sides of the cake. Ensure the grooves are smooth and solid without any air bubbles. If not perfect the first time, keep going around until you are happy with them.

Tidy up the top of the cake by spreading the overlapping buttercream from the edge towards the middle, then chill for about 20 minutes until the buttercream has set.

Spoon 2–3 heaped tbsp of the buttercream into a piping bag fitted with a small star nozzle and set aside – this will be used for piping the rosettes.

Divide the remaining buttercream into 2 portions – one portion should be twice the amount of the second portion. Mix the larger amount to a light pink and the smaller amount to a light brown using the corresponding food colourings. Spoon each colour into a piping bag.

Remove the cake from the fridge and place it back on the turntable. Snip about 1cm (½in) off the tip of each piping bag and use them to fill the grooves left by the comb – the pink buttercream should fill the top and bottom grooves and the brown should fill the middle groove. The buttercreams should overflow the gaps a little to prevent any air pockets from forming.

Dip a metal side scraper in warm water, dry it on a cloth, and scrape it around the cake to smoothen the sides and remove any excess coloured buttercream. Apply a fair amount of pressure when doing so to ensure the stripes will be sharp and clean.

Using the piping bag with the plain buttercream that you set aside, pipe 10 evenly-sized and -spaced out rosettes around the top of the cake.

Decorate each rosette with a large pink pearlised choco ball and finish with a small sugar snowflake sprinkles and the metallic mini sugar pearls.

The Basics

In this chapter you will find a selection of recipes and techniques referred to throughout this book.

My easy-to-use basic sugar cookie dough provides a perfect cookie base which lends itself to any style of decoration and can be flavoured to your liking. You will also find my recipe for half & half paste (a slightly firmer version of sugar paste), which I use for lots of sugar decorations in the book.

For cakes, you will find my tried and tested chiffon sponge recipe. It's super light and fluffy and works so well with delicate meringue buttercreams and fruit purées; its simplicity is what makes it so essential, allowing the cake fillings to really shine. The buttermilk sponge is a hugely useful base for almost any cake; it will be moist and soft and is very easy to bake, making it perfect for layer cakes as well as cupcakes. You can make either of these a day in advance and store them wrapped in cling film overnight. I find that this intensifies the flavours and firms up the crumb, making the cakes easier to work with the next day. I have also included a step-by-step guide with images on how to layer and mask a cake.

My basic cream cheese frosting is very moreish and tastes delicious as a cake filling as well as a frosting for cupcakes, especially with chocolate, red velvet or buttermilk cake. I use meringue buttercream for lots of my cakes and cupcakes; it is beautifully smooth and holds up very well, even at room temperature. It's very pale in colour making it perfect for adding colour or fruit purées. The technique requires a little practice and patience and it is imperative that all the steps and instructions are followed precisely and the correct equipment is used. It's best used freshly made, without chilling, for a perfectly glossy and smooth finish.

Lastly, the meringue kisses are made from a nice and stable, glossy meringue that can be coloured and flavoured as you like.

I hope that you will find the recipes in this book useful and that it will be a go-to reference for many happy baking years to come. We would absolutely love to see any of your creations and if you'd like to share, please do tag us @peggyporschenofficial on Instagram.

Basic equipment

If, like me, you have a real love for the art of baking and decorating, it's important to start with the basics when striving for professional results. Investing in a set of good-quality specialist items will not only give your baking masterpieces a real edge, but it will also last for years. You can build your toolkit over time by cross-referencing what you need with the recipe you are working on. To get you on your way, here are the specialist items that I use on a regular basis, along with some kitchen essentials.

FOR GENERAL BAKING (CAKES & CUPCAKES)

Electric mixer (preferably a free-standing mixer with attachments such as a paddle and whisk)

3 x 15cm (6in) round shallow cake tins – I use these for all my layer cakes. Using 3 shallow tins rather than one deep tin ensures that the sponges bake more evenly and retain more moisture. Baking the whole sponge in one deep tin can dry it out around the edges while the centre risks being underbaked.

2 baking trays

Baking parchment

Oil spray

Cling film

Kitchen cloth

2 wire cooling racks

Selection of mixing bowls

Selection of jugs

2 x 12-hole cupcake baking trays

Rubber spatula

Balloon whisk

Kitchen scales (preferably a digital one that weighs in 1g or 2g units)

Measuring jugs and/or measuring cups

Selection of small and large kitchen knives, plain-edged and serrated

Pair of scissors

Selection of saucepans

Stick blender

Sugar or jam thermometer

Selection of sieves (strainers)

Pastry brush

Large rolling pin

Storage containers

FOR LAYERING & ICING CAKES & PIPING CUPCAKES

Cake turntable (I recommend Ateco)

Non-slip mat (you can find these online from Ateco or Nisbets)

Cake disc (eg the loose base of a 30cm/12in cake tin)

Large palette knife

Cake leveller

Ruler

Cake side scraper (preferably metal)

Buttercream comb

Large piping bag (you can use fabric or plastic; I recommend biodegradable ones if using plastic)

Selection of small, large, round and star-shaped piping nozzles

Melon baller or apple corer

FOR DECORATING COOKIES & MAKING SUGAR DECORATIONS

Small rolling pin

Non-stick plastic board (with non-slip mat)

Various cutters and silicone moulds

Flower foam pad

Colour mixing palette

Mini palette knife

Selection of artist's brushes in different sizes, flat and fine

Paper piping bags made from waxed parchment paper (or use a small plastic one with a small round nozzle if required)

Pair of tweezers

Cocktail sticks (toothpicks)

Basic Sugar Cookie Dough

200g (7oz/¾ cup plus 2 tbsp) unsalted butter, softened
200g (7oz/1 cup) caster sugar
flavouring of choice (or as shown in the cookie recipe)
pinch of salt
1 medium egg, at room temperature
400g (14oz/3 cups) plain (all-purpose) flour, plus extra
   for dusting

**Specialist equipment (see page 164 for a basic
   equipment list and page 182 for stockists)**
Cookie cutter(s)

Preheat the oven to 175°C fan/375°F/Gas 5 and
line 2 baking trays with baking parchment.

Place the butter, sugar, your flavouring of choice
and the salt into the mixing bowl of an electric mixer
fitted with a paddle attachment and cream
together until smooth and creamy in texture.

Beat the egg lightly and slowly add it to the butter
mixture while beating until fully incorporated.

Sift the flour and gradually add it to the mixture until
just combined.

Bring together to form a dough, then wrap it in cling
film and chill for at least 30 minutes until the dough
feels firm and cool. It is now ready to use in the
specific recipe.

TO BAKE THE COOKIES

Once cool, unwrap the dough and briefly knead it
through to soften it slightly.

Place onto a lightly floured smooth work surface
and roll it out to the required thickness, as stated in
the recipe.

Using a cookie cutter, stamp out the required
shapes and place them onto the lined baking trays,
spaced at least 1cm (½in) apart. Ensure that there
are no wrinkles in the paper under the cookies and
weigh the edges of the paper down if using a
fan-assisted oven, otherwise the cookies may lift
up during the baking process and turn out uneven.
You can gather up any big off-cuts of dough and
re-roll to stamp out more shapes but don't do this
too many times otherwise the dough will become
tough. Put the trays of cookies in the fridge to chill
for about 10 minutes.

Bake for 8–12 minutes, turning the trays once
during baking to ensure they bake evenly. When
cooked, they should look golden brown and spring
back when pressing down with your finger. Allow the
cookies to cool on the tray.

Half & Half Paste

Half & half paste is made of equal quantities of sugar paste (also called fondant) and sugar florist paste (also called gum paste or flower paste). Sugar paste is typically used to cover cakes and remains soft enough to cut, while sugar florist paste sets hard once dry. By mixing both of them together, you will get a soft yet pliable textured paste that doesn't stretch too much when handled and is still soft enough to eat once dry, making it perfect for icing cookies. The quantity below is the average amount required for the iced cookie recipes in this book. For larger or smaller amounts, simply adjust the weights, always using equal quantities of each paste.

300g (10½oz) white sugar florist paste
a small amount of white vegetable fat (eg Trex)
300g (10½oz) white sugar paste
food colouring paste of choice, if required

Unwrap the sugar florist paste and check it for any dry and crumbly pieces; trim them off with a knife to ensure they don't get mixed into the paste as they will spoil the whole batch.

Rub a small amount of white vegetable fat between your hands before kneading the florist paste until smooth. Should the paste stick, add a little more vegetable fat.

Wrap the florist paste in cling film and set aside. It sets very quickly if exposed to air. Wrap immediately when not using it to avoid cracked or brittle paste.

Repeat the first 2 steps above for the sugar paste.

Unwrap the florist paste and mix it together with the sugar paste until smooth and flexible. The paste should feel soft and stretchy.

If using food colouring, take a small amount of half & half paste and mix it with some food colouring to a darker shade than required. Ensure that the colouring has completely blended with the paste. Add the coloured paste back into the main batch, a little at a time, and mix until you have achieved the required shade. Paste colours usually darken slightly after a little while, so it's better to finish with a slightly lighter shade of colour than required and rest the paste for half an hour. If still too pale, add a little more of the coloured paste later.

Wrap the paste in cling film and rest for about 10 minutes to allow it to firm up slightly before using.

TIPS

Always keep your paste covered with cling film when not using, as it can dry quickly. Do not mix dry bits back into it, as they will make the texture lumpy. Trim them off instead. To store your paste for a longer time, first wrap it in cling film, then place it in an airtight container or thick freezer bag. Cling film alone is not sufficient for long-term storage.

Try not to overwork florist paste. If kneading it for too long in your bare hands the fatty acids of your skin can make the paste brittle and tough after a while. To prevent this, wear thin rubber gloves.

If you have warm hands and the paste gets sticky when kneading it, use a cool marble or granite top to work on and keep hand contact to a minimum. Dab a little cornflour on your hands to absorb the moisture if required, but not too much as it can make your paste brittle.

Royal Icing

500g (1lb 2oz/3½ cups) icing (confectioner's) sugar,
  sifted
2 egg whites
squeeze of lemon juice (optional)
food colouring paste of choice, if required

Put the icing sugar into the bowl of an electric mixer fitted with a paddle attachment. (The bowl and paddle should be spotlessly clean and grease-free.)

In a separate bowl, lightly beat the egg whites, then pour about three-quarters of them into the icing sugar. Start mixing at low speed until combined. Scrape down the sides and bottom of the bowl using a rubber spatula and make sure the icing is well combined. Ensure you clean the spatula after each use to not contaminate the icing with dry bits.

Add the lemon juice, if using, and mix for 2 minutes at the lowest setting. If the mixture looks too dry and grainy, add some more egg white until the icing looks smooth but not wet around the sides of the bowl. Scrape the sides and bottom down again and continue mixing for about 5 minutes until the icing forms stiff peaks and you can hear a 'sloshing' sound as the paddle moves around.

Stop mixing. Dip the spatula into the icing, lift it and hold it up. If the icing forms a stiff peak that holds, it's ready.

Transfer the icing to a clean, dry storage container (avoid picking up any dry bits from the paddle or the edge of the bowl) and cover the icing with a damp (not wet) cloth. Seal with a lid or cling film. Store for up to 1 week at room temperature. The egg white and icing sugar may separate – simply put the mix back into the bowl and whip up for a couple of minutes at low speed using the paddle attachment.

COLOURING ROYAL ICING

Put 1 tbsp royal icing into a bowl. Using a cocktail stick (toothpick), add a small amount of food colouring paste.

Blend together with a small palette knife, making sure that you break down any tiny specks of colour as these will cause bleeding if not combined properly. Mix the icing to a slightly darker shade than the required colour.

Little by little, add the coloured icing back into the main batch of icing, mixing well each time, until you have achieved the required shade.

Note: you should always mix your royal icing with colouring first (if required) before adding water to change the consistency.

CONSISTENCIES

In the book I refer to 2 consistencies: 'soft-peak', which is used for piping outlines and details, and 'flooding', which is for covering large areas.

For a soft-peak piping consistency

Place the required amount of royal icing into a small bowl. Dip a small palette knife in water and mix it through the icing. Keep adding a few drops of water at a time and continue mixing through the icing with a palette knife until the texture becomes slightly glossy and the peaks start falling over. The consistency should be similar to that of toothpaste.

For flooding consistency

Follow the instructions for 'soft-peak', then continue adding water until the icing flows together and flattens out after 4–6 seconds.

Paper Piping Bag

Learning how to fashion a homemade paper piping bag is a useful lesson for any baker. I fill the piping bag with royal icing to pipe very small details onto cookies, for example. If this is your first time making a paper piping bag, it may take a little practice, but don't give up, as the results make it well worth sticking with. Make sure that your scissors are sharp, and don't fray the edges of the paper when cutting, as this can result in the icing curling when piping.

waxed parchment paper
scissors

Take a rectangular piece of waxed parchment paper, approximately 30 x 45cm (12 x 17½in), and cut it in half diagonally from one corner to the opposite corner. For a clean cut, slide the scissors through the paper instead of making small snips or using a knife. A sharp paper edge will make a neat piping tip.

You should now have 2 paper triangles, each with a long corner, a short corner and one right angle (90 degrees).

Hold one of the resulting triangles with one hand at the right-angled corner. With the other hand, bring the short corner up to the right-angled corner, curving the paper inwards so it forms a loose cone. Hold both paper corners with one hand.

With your other hand, grab the long corner and wrap it around the cone shape twice. As you wrap the paper around the cone for the second time, bring the third corner up to join the other 2. As you do this the cone will tighten and the tip should close up. If not fully closed, you can tighten and close the tip up by adjusting all 3 corners with your hands.

Once closed, fold all 3 corners over to the inside of the cone, twice, to form a firm edge that doesn't unfold easily.

Prepare as many piping bags as you need. Only ever half-fill them with icing otherwise the contents will ooze out of the top when you squeeze. Once half-filled, flatten the upper part of the piping bag with the seam of the paper in the middle. Fold the paper, over and away from the seam, and keep folding down until the bag feels firmly filled. This tension will make the piping process easier.

When ready, simply snip a small hole off the tip and start piping. Ensure you keep the fold firmly closed as you squeeze out the icing to maintain pressure on the bag and to prevent the icing from oozing out at the top. Keep piping bags that are filled with royal icing in a plastic bag or cling film to prevent the icing from drying.

Buttermilk Sponge

MAKES A 15CM (6IN) LAYER CAKE OR 24 CUPCAKES

For a layer cake
65g (2¼ oz/¼ cup plus 1 tsp) unsalted butter
65g (2¼ oz/¼ cup plus 1 tsp) salted butter
330g (11¾oz/1¾ cups less 1½ tbsp) caster sugar
1 large egg
300g (10½oz/2¼ cups) plain (all-purpose) flour
300g (10½oz/1¼ cups) buttermilk
flavouring (refer to cake recipe)
1½ tsp bicarbonate of soda (baking soda)
1½ tsp white wine vinegar
sugar syrup (refer to cake recipe)

Specialist equipment (see page 164 for a basic equipment list and page 182 for stockists)
3 x 15cm (6in) shallow cake tins
oil spray

For cupcakes
85g (3oz/⅓ cup plus 2 tsp) unsalted butter
85g (3oz/⅓ cup plus 2 tsp) salted butter
440g (15½oz/2¼ cups less 1 tbsp) caster sugar
2 small eggs
400g (14oz/3 cups) plain (all-purpose) flour
400g (14oz/1¾ cups) buttermilk
flavouring (refer to cupcake recipe)
2 tsp bicarbonate of soda (baking soda)
2 tsp white wine vinegar
sugar syrup (refer to cake recipe)

Specialist equipment (see page 164 for a basic equipment list and page 182 for stockists)
2 x 12-hole cupcake baking trays
24 paper baking cases

Preheat the oven to 175°C fan/375°F/Gas 5. Grease 3 x 15cm (6in) shallow cake tins with oil spray and line the bases with baking parchment. For cupcakes, line 2 x 12-hole cupcake trays with baking cases.

Put both butters and the sugar into the bowl of an electric mixer fitted with a paddle attachment and cream together until pale and fluffy. This will take a while, so do this as a first step to allow plenty of time to aerate the mixture.

Lightly beat the eggs in a separate bowl, then slowly pour them into the butter and sugar mix while beating on medium speed. Watch as the eggs combine with the butter mix and stop pouring if the batter needs time to come together, then add more. The eggs and butter should both be at room temperature to avoid splitting. However, should the mixture split, add 1 tbsp flour to bring the batter back together before adding more egg.

Add the flour and buttermilk to the batter in alternate batches and mix until combined. Add the required flavouring to the batter and mix in.

Mix the vinegar and bicarbonate of soda together and immediately, as it bubbles, add it to the batter.

For a layer cake, evenly divide the batter between the 3 prepared cake tins. For cupcakes, fill a large piping bag with the batter and snip 2.5cm (1in) off the tip. Pipe the batter into the baking cases, filling each one about two-thirds full.

Bake the layer cakes for about 30–35 minutes and the cupcakes for about 15 minutes, depending on your oven. The sponges are cooked when golden and the tops spring back to the touch.

Leave the sponges to rest in the tins for a few minutes and brush the tops with the sugar syrup. This will prevent the cakes from forming a hard crust and the heat will ensure the moisture and flavour are absorbed easily. If stated in the recipe, reserve the remainder of the syrup for layering.

Remove the sponge layers from the tins using a small knife to release the sides, or take the cupcakes out of the trays. Wipe the bottoms of the cupcakes with a damp cloth if sticky from the syrup. Allow to cool completely on a wire rack.

Chiffon Sponge

105g (3½oz) egg yolks (from approx. 6 eggs)
300g (10½oz/1½ cups) caster sugar
flavouring (refer to cake recipe)
100ml (3½ fl oz/7 tbsp) sunflower oil
300g (10½oz/2¼ cups) plain (all-purpose) flour
4 tsp baking powder

220g (7¾oz) egg whites (from approx. 7 eggs)
160ml (5½fl oz/⅔ cup) whole milk

Specialist equipment (see page 164 for a basic equipment list and page 182 for stockists)
3 x 15cm (6in) shallow cake tins

Preheat the oven to 175°C fan/375°F/Gas 5. Grease 3 x 15cm (6in) shallow cake tins with oil spray and line the bases with baking parchment.

Put the egg yolks, sugar and flavouring into the bowl of an electric mixer fitted with a whisk attachment and whisk on medium-high speed until pale and fluffy.

While still whisking, slowly add the sunflower oil.

Sift together the flour and baking powder in a bowl.

In a separate electric mixer bowl, whisk the egg white using a whisk attachment on medium speed until fluffy.

Alternating between the 2, add the flour and the milk to the egg-sugar mixture in batches and mix until combined.

Gently and carefully fold the egg white into the batter, making sure not to lose the aeration of the batter.

Divide the batter evenly between the 3 prepared cake tins, no more than three-quarters full.

Bake the cakes for 20–30 minutes until a nice golden colour. The sponge is cooked if it shrinks away from the sides of the tin and the top springs back to the touch. It will rise quite high while it's baking but will sink down a bit when cooled.

Turn each cake, along with its cake tin, upside down onto a baking tray lined with baking parchment and leave to cool for about 20 minutes with the tin on top of the cake. This helps to prevent the sponge from sinking in the middle and ensures an even depth and texture.

Unmould from the tins, using a small knife to release the cakes around the edges and leave to cool completely on a wire rack.

Assembling a Cake
LAYERING, CRUMB COATING & MASKING

3 sponge cake layers
sugar syrup (if required)
cake filling (if required)
buttercream or frosting (at room temperature)

Specialist equipment (see page 164 for a basic equipment list and page 182 for stockists)
turntable (preferably with a non-slip top or damp cloth)

cake disc (needs to be a few inches larger than the cake board – I use the loose base of a 30cm/12in cake tin)
long serrated knife or cake leveller
ruler
large palette knife
plain-edge side scraper
tall jug filled with hot water
kitchen cloth
15cm (6in) thin cake board

Have all your tools and equipment ready and set up at your work station before you start.

See step-by-step pictures on pages 174 and 175 for the following instructions.

Trim the tops off each sponge layer using a long serrated kitchen knife or cake leveller. Ensure that each sponge layer is even in height. If using a cake leveller, you can adjust the height of the wire using a ruler. Each sponge layer should be around 2.5cm (1in) high.

Also trim the bottom off one of the sponge layers only – this will be the middle layer.

Place the cake disc on top of your turntable. If you don't have one with a non-slip top, dampen a thin kitchen cloth and place it between the turntable and cake disc.

Spread a dab of buttercream onto the middle of the disc, then place the 15cm (6in) cake board on top. Chill for a few minutes to set the buttercream (if you have a non-slip mat, you can use this instead of the buttercream to hold the cake board in place).

Spread a thin layer of buttercream in the middle of the cake board and place the first sponge layer on top, with the crumb (bottom) side facing down.

Brush the sponge with the sugar syrup, if required in the recipe.

Using a palette knife, spread a layer of filling or buttercream (depending on the recipe) evenly on top of the sponge, about 5mm (¼in) thick, or fill as instructed in the recipe.

Place the middle sponge layer on top (the one that has been trimmed on both sides) and repeat the steps above to soak it with syrup, if required, and spread it with buttercream.

Place the third sponge on top, this time crumb side up, and brush the top with syrup, if required.

Ensure that all the sponges are centred and the top of the cake is level. Tidy up any bits of buttercream that are squeezing out from around the edges with a palette knife. If the sponge layers and cake filling are very soft and slide around, transfer the cake (on the cake disc) to the fridge to set for about 20 minutes before applying the crumb coat.

To crumb coat the cake, spoon about 2–3 heaped tbsp of the buttercream on top of the cake. Gently spread it from the middle of the cake towards the edges, until the top is evenly coated and level.

Spread more buttercream around the sides until completely covered. Smoothen and straighten the sides using the side scraper. Hold the straight edge of the side scraper in a perfectly vertical position against the cake and angle it away by about 45 degrees. Go around in one long swoop as you spin the turntable in the opposite direction to your hand motion.

Clean up the top of the cake by spreading the excess buttercream from the edge towards the middle of the cake using the palette knife or side scraper.

The reason this first coat is called the 'crumb coat' is because its purpose is to hold the crumbs in place and create a solid basic shape. It doesn't have to be perfect and it's fine if some cake crumb shows through the buttercream.

Transfer the cake (including the cake disc) back into the fridge and chill for at least 30 minutes, or until the crumb coat has set.

Once the crumb coat has set, repeat the previous crumb coating instructions to mask the cake with a perfectly smooth and even layer of buttercream (unless stated otherwise in the recipe) and chill again until set.

TIPS

It's always handy to have a bowl with hot water and a cloth on the side to dip and clean the palette knife or metal side scraper between smoothening actions. This will help make the buttercream nice and smooth.

When serving cakes, I recommend taking them out of the fridge at least 30–60 minutes (depending on room temperature) before eating them. Cold cake can taste dry and prevent the flavours from coming through.

To slice a cake, I suggest using a long, plain-edged kitchen knife. Dip it in a jug of hot water frequently between slices and dry it with a cloth before cutting into the cake.

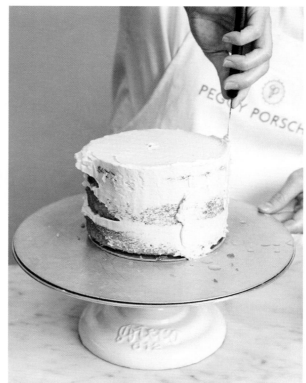

Meringue Buttercream

For a layer cake

270g (9½oz/1¼ cups plus 2 tbsp) caster sugar
65ml (2fl oz/¼ cup plus 1 tsp) water
150g (5½oz) egg whites (from approx. 5 eggs)
340g (11¾oz/1½ cups) unsalted butter, diced and
  softened
flavouring, such as fruit purée or caramel, if required
  in recipe

For cupcakes

430g (15oz/2 cups plus 2 tbsp) caster sugar
100ml (3½fl oz/scant ½ cup) water
240g (8½oz) egg whites (from approx. 8 eggs)
540g (1lb 3oz/2⅓ cups) unsalted butter, diced and
  softened
flavouring, such as fruit purée or caramel, if required
  in recipe

Put the sugar and water in a small saucepan and bring to a boil, stirring occasionally. Place a sugar thermometer in the pan.

Put the egg whites into the bowl of an electric mixer fitted with a whisk attachment. (Ensure the bowl and whisk are grease free or the meringue will not whip up properly.)

Once the sugar reaches 116°C/240°F, start whisking the egg whites to a stiff peak on the lowest speed.

Once the sugar reaches 121°C/250°F (softball stage), remove the pan from the heat.

Slowly pour the hot syrup into the whipped egg whites in a thin and steady stream (also called 'string pouring') while still mixing on a low to medium speed. Once all the sugar syrup is added, turn the speed up to high and continue whisking until the mixture has cooled to lukewarm and the meringue is stiff and fluffy.

Now slowly add the soft, diced butter to the meringue, a few cubes at a time and whisking all the time, until it is all incorporated. The texture should look smooth and glossy. If it looks split, continue whisking as it may take some time to come together.

Add the flavouring and/or fruit purées required for the recipe, if applicable and mix through.

If not using it immediately, transfer the buttercream to an airtight container or bowl covered with cling film and store in the fridge for up to a week.

To bring the buttercream back to a soft layering or piping texture, put it into the microwave and heat it in short bursts of 10 seconds at a time, mixing with a whisk in between bursts until it is soft enough to use.

TROUBLESHOOTING

If your buttercream splits, this could be for 2 reasons – the butter is either too cold or too warm.

If the butter is too cold, use a blowtorch or bain marie to warm up the outside of the bowl so that the temperature of the meringue and butter are more similar and they will come back together.

If the butter is too warm, place the split buttercream in the fridge or freezer for a couple of minutes so that the buttercream firms up. Go back to whisking and it should come back together.

Note: During the process of adding the butter, the mixture will look split at some point. But don't worry as this is the fat being emulsified with the meringue to achieve a smooth glossy buttercream. Just keep whisking!

Cream Cheese Frosting

MAKES 1.2KG (2.5LBS) OR ENOUGH TO PIPE 24 CUPCAKES

270g (9½oz/1¼ cups) full-fat cream cheese, preferably
  Philadelphia
300g (10½oz/1⅓ cups) unsalted butter, softened
650g (1lb 7oz/4¾ cups) icing (confectioner's) sugar,
  sifted
flavouring, if required
food colouring, if required

Put the cream cheese into the bowl of an electric mixer fitted with a paddle attachment and cream until smooth.

In a separate bowl, cream together the butter and icing sugar until pale and fluffy.

Add the cream cheese to the butter mixture in batches and beat until well combined.

Add the required flavouring and mix until well combined.

If adding food colour, mix 1 tbsp of the frosting with a small amount of food colouring to a darker shade of colour than required. Blend together with a palette knife until all the colour specks have dissolved.

Little by little, add the coloured frosting back into the main batch and mix until you have reached the shade you require.

Cover the bowl with either a lid or cling film and chill until set.

FIND & COLLECT PROPS

One of my favourite styling features is what I think of as 'the props'. I believe this is a passion that grows over time. My husband Bryn calls me a hoarder, but I adore squirrelling away a collection of treasures that will, at some point, come in handy. For example, I love vintage cake stands and crockery. I'm also obsessed with small ornaments, pretty ribbons and beautiful fabrics.

When it comes to building your own collection, you need to think like a magpie, and always be on the lookout for anything that catches your eye. Sometimes a delicate pattern on a table linen or a tea cup can inspire a new cake design or seasonal collection. I find great enjoyment in hunting through antique stores, charity shops and vintage fairs, both here in the UK and abroad. My advice would be to think of all the seasons when you are looking, regardless of the one you are currently in.

Fruit Purée

Fruit purées make delicious cupcake fillings or flavourings for buttercream, for example. You can use fresh or frozen fruit, however fresh is preferable as it has more flavour, is brighter in colour, and contains less water. Always remove stones, kernels and stalks before weighing out the required amount and wash the fruit before cooking. I recommend having a fine-mesh sieve and a rubber spatula to hand for making purées. To achieve the right consistency, you need to thoroughly scrape all the pulp from the cooked fruit, which is easiest to do with a rubber spatula. Here is a guide to the ratios and consistencies for the different fruits used in the book.

Strawberries, Raspberries and Blackberries

Ratio: Double the weight of berries versus the required weight of purée. For example, cook 200g (7oz) berries to make 100g (3½oz) purée.

Consistency: Should coat the back of a spoon, similar to runny honey.

Blueberries

Ratio: 30% more berries than the required weight of purée. For example, cook 130g (4½oz) berries to make 100g (3½oz) purée.

Consistency: Thicker than, for example, raspberry purée, similar to smooth apple sauce.

Cherries

Ratio: Triple the weight of cherries versus the required weight of purée. For example, cook 300g (10½oz) cherries to make about 100g (3½oz) purée.

Consistency: Runny at first, but cook the purée for about another 15 minutes after removing the skins until the liquid has reduced down and the consistency is somewhere between that of runny honey and apple sauce.

Wash the fruit and remove any stones, kernels or stalks.

Chop the fruit into small pieces and put into a saucepan together with 1 tbsp water. Cover with a lid.

Bring to a gentle boil, stirring occasionally, and cook until the fruit turns mushy.

Remove from the heat and allow to cool slightly.

Blend the cooked fruit with a stick blender or crush with a fork until the fruit turns to a thick purée.

Pass the purée through a fine-mesh sieve, pressing it through the sieve with a rubber spatula into a small bowl, to remove any pips or pieces of skin. Ensure that all the pulp has been pushed through and scrape any that's left on the back of the sieve.

Weigh to check if you have the required amount (and consistency). If it is too runny, continue to cook a little longer to reduce the purée down.

Allow to cool completely.

Meringue Kisses

100g (3½oz) egg whites (from approx. 3 eggs)
100g (3½oz/½ cup) caster sugar
100g (3½oz/¾ cup) icing (confectioner's) sugar, sifted
flavouring, if required in recipe
food colouring, if required in recipe

**Specialist equipment (see page 164 for a basic
    equipment list and page 182 for stockists)**
large piping bag fitted with the required nozzle

Preheat the oven to 80°C/175°F/Gas ¼ and line 2 baking trays with baking parchment.

Put the egg whites and sugar into a metal or glass heatproof bowl and whisk together with a balloon whisk. Place the bowl over a hot water bath (bain marie) and continue whisking until the meringue becomes white and fluffy and it reaches 55°C/131°F on a sugar thermometer.

Once the temperature is reached, transfer the meringue to the bowl of an electric mixer fitted with a whisk attachment and whisk at medium speed until cool.

Once the meringue is cool, gradually add the icing sugar and continue whisking until fully combined and stiff.

At this point, add any flavourings that the recipe requires, if applicable.

If adding food colouring, mix 1 tbsp of the meringue with the colour paste to a deeper shade than required. Blend together with a palette knife until all the colour specks have dispersed.

Little by little, mix the coloured meringue back into the main batch of meringue until you have reached the required colour.

To make meringue kisses, spoon the meringue into a piping bag fitted with a round or star nozzle. Stick the baking parchment onto a baking tray with blobs of meringue in each corner to prevent it from lifting if using a fan-assisted oven.

Pipe the meringue kisses onto the prepared trays with at least 1cm (½in) between each one and bake for about 1 hour, or until the meringues can be lifted clean off the tray. Allow to cool.

If stored in an airtight container the kisses will last for up to 4 weeks.

Decorations, equipment & suppliers

DECORATIONS

Colours and tints

Some suppliers offer edible as well as craft-only colours. Please use only colours and tints that are suitable for consumption to make the cakes and cookies in this book.

gold edible lustre powder (eg antique gold from Sugarflair)
gold edible lustre spray (from PME)
pearl edible lustre spray (from PME)
black edible food pen (from Rainbow Dust)
blush pink blossom tint (from Sugarflair)
edible gold lustre dust (eg from Sugarflair)
dusky pink food colouring paste (from Sugarflair)
ice blue food colouring paste (from Sugarflair)
yellow, pink, green and black food colouring pastes (eg Primrose, Fuchsia, Peppermint and Black Extra from Sugarflair)
pink or purple and yellow food colouring pastes (eg Fuchsia or Magenta and Primrose from Sugarflair)

Sprinkles and decorations

pink & red mini glimmer sugar hearts (from Twist Ingredients)
matt 100s & 1000s red & pink mix (from Twist Ingredients)
silver metallic mini sugar pearls (from Twist Ingredients)
small pink glimmer pearls (from Twist Ingredients)
popping candy (from Heston at Waitrose)
pink pearlescent choco balls (from Twist Ingredients)
mini sugar snowflakes (from Culpitt)
sprinkles (eg snowflakes, pink, silver and metallic mini sugar pearls from Twist Ingredients)
mini meringue kisses, eg 'Meringue Drops' (from FunCakes)
Bordeaux glimmer 100s & 1000s (from Twist Ingredients)
sugar decorations (eg silver star sprinkles, silver macaroni rods, pink glimmer vermicelli, pink and silver mini sugar pearls, pink metallic pearls, 4mm from Twist Ingredients)
large pearlescent choco balls in pink, blue and ivory (from Twist Ingredients)
small silver and pink metallic sugar pearls (from Twist Ingredients)

Edible flowers

freeze-dried edible rose petals (from Uncle Roy's)
10 pale pink wafer rose buds (from Culpitt)
10 pale green wafer leaves (from Culpitt)
dehydrated edible petals, eg yellow calendula, blue cornflower, pink carnation, orange marigold (from Uncle Roy's and DG Store UK)

Flavours

lemon essence (from Uncle Roy's)
natural blueberry essence (from Uncle Roy's)
peppermint essence (from Uncle Roy's)
elderflower essence (from Uncle Roy's)

EQUIPMENT

bee silicone mould (mine is from a Butterfly & Insect Brooch Mould by Karen Davies)
15cm (6in) shallow cake tins (eg from Alan Silverwood)
rose wax seal stamp (I found mine on Amazon)
primrose blossom cutter and veiner set (eg from Blossom Sugar Art)
Easter chick cookie cutter (mine came from a set called 'Chick with Bow Tie' by Wilton)
mini tulip cutter (mine is from an Easter cookie cutter set by R & M International)
interlocking circles stencil (eg from Designer Stencils)
bevelled cake comb (from a set of patterned-edge side scrapers by PME)
medium and large toadstool cookie cutter (I found mine at Cutter Craft)
medium and large gills stencil set (I had mine custom made by Cuttersweet)
rose stems silicone mould (from Katy Sue Designs)
pumpkin face stencil (I had mine custom made by Cuttersweet)
Dresden or veining tool (from PME or JEM)
small ghost cutter and ghost cookie cutter set (from Cutter Craft)
BOO lettering stamps (part of the 'Vanilla Set' by Sweets Stamp)
XXL snowman cookie cutter (from RBV Birkmann)
cable silicone mould (from Katy Sue Designs)
rustic cable knit mould (from Karen Davies)
gingerbread house cutter set (from Dexam – comes with various cutters you won't need for this project but contains the door and heart)
deer/fawn cookie cutter, 6cm (from Staedter)
small christmas tree cookie cutter, 6cm (from RBV Birkmann)
mini snowflake plunger cutter (from a set by PME)
fine-toothed side scraper (mine is from a set by PME)
small polar bear cutter (mine is from a set by Cutter Craft)
stripe contour comb (from Evil Cake Genius or Wilton)
foldable cinnamon star cutter (eg from Staedter)

UK & EUROPEAN SUPPLIERS & STOCKISTS

Sugarflair – sugarflair.com
Trade/wholesale supplier for food colourings. Products are widely available on Amazon and from various specialist sugarcraft suppliers.

Cuttersweet – cuttersweet.com
Large range of cookie cutters and stencils, including custom designs.

PME – pmecake.com
Cake decorating equipment such as piping nozzles (including JEM) and edible lustre spray.

Twist Ingredients – twistingredients.co.uk
Edible decorations and sprinkles.

Alan Silverwood – silverwood-bakeware.com
Award-winning professional-grade bakeware designed and made in Birmingham, UK.

Culpitt – culpitt.com
Trade/wholesale supplier for all things baking and cake decorating. Products are widely available on Amazon and from various specialist sugarcraft suppliers.

Squires Kitchen Shop – squires-shop.com
Great brand for sugar florist paste and reliable source for all things cake decorating and sugarcraft.

Uncle Roy's – uncleroys.co.uk
Large variety of good-quality extracts and dried edible flowers.

Karen Davies – karendaviessugarcraft.co.uk
Extensive range of beautiful silicone sugar moulds.

Katy Sue Designs – katysuedesigns.com
Extensive range of beautiful silicone sugar moulds.

SweetStamp – sweetstamp.online
Artist's brushes, letter stamps and slogans.

Sous Chef – souschef.co.uk
Biodegradable piping bags, specialist tools and ingredients.

Rainbow Dust – rainbowdust.co.uk
Food colours and edible food pens.

Blossom Sugar Art – blossomsugarart.com
Flower cutters and moulds.

RBV Birkmann – birkmann.de
Bakeware and cookie cutter supplier based in Germany, also available in the UK.

Staedter – staedter.de
Bakeware and cookie cutter (cinnamon stars) supplier based in Germany, also available in the UK.

Cutter Craft – cuttercraft.co.uk
Great for unique cookie cutter shapes.

DG Store UK – dgstoreuk.com
For edible flowers and spices.

R&M International – morethanbaking.com
For a wide selection of cookie cutters.

Pineapple Circus – pineapplecircus.co.uk
For silk flowers.

Covent Garden Flower Market – newcoventgardenmarket.com
For silk and fresh flowers.

Wilms – wilms-aachen.de/
Seasonal decorations and flowers based in Germany.

Peggy at Home – peggyporschen.com
For Peggy's range of baking kits, aprons and specialist equipment.

US SUPPLIERS & STOCKISTS

Evil Cake Genius – evilcakegenius.com
Fantastic range of cake and cookie stencils.

Ateco – atecousa.com
Turntables and general pastry equipment.

Global Sugar Art – globalsugarart.com
Great range of cake decorating supplies.

Sweetapolita – sweetapolita.com
Beautiful range of sugar sprinkles.

Copper Gifts – coppergifts.com
Hand-made copper cookie cutters in all shapes and sizes.

Wilton – wilton.com
Probably the world's best-known manufacturer and supplier of baking and cake decorating equipment as well as edible decorations.

Designer Stencils – designerstencils.com
US-based manufacturer of cake and cookie stencils. Available in the UK from cakedecoratingcompany.com

Index

Acknowledgements

I have always been a great believer in teamwork and bouncing off one another to come up with the best ideas. I think of myself as someone who has the ability to bring together talented, like-minded people to join me on my journey and help me create and bring my vision to reality. This book is no exception and it has been the hard work, dedication and accumulation of lots of wonderful recipes, ideas and collections we have created at and for the Peggy Porschen Parlour over the recent years. While most of my previous books I have written and themed around a certain subject or cake category, this book is a little bit different.

Back in 2015, having released my ninth book *Love Layer Cakes*, I decided to take a break from writing in order to focus on building and evolving the Peggy Porschen Parlour brand. The Parlour's transition to stardom began around Christmas 2016 when we first created a pastel Christmas theme. Breaking from traditional Christmas colours, the collection featured pink Santas and we decorated our Belgravia Parlour with pastel baubles and lots of twinkling lights. It was an instant success and by Summer 2017, I started to truly embrace our new-found identity and a pattern began to emerge. It became evident that there was a natural synergy between our seasonal offerings and the artistic storytelling woven throughout our installations. This book *A Year in Cake* is a 'best of' from all the wonderful seasons we celebrate throughout the year at our dreamy boutique bakery. It features our most iconic, well-loved, tried and tested recipes and designs we have developed since our Parlour journey took off.

I have been lucky enough that the following people have crossed my path, opened my eyes, widened my horizon and taught me to believe in myself and in my brand and to push boundaries. These people have inspired me to grow and continue to do so.

Firstly, I'd like to thank my publisher of 15 years (!) Quadrille, in particular my editor Céline Hughes and designer Alicia House for working with me on creating this beautiful book. This is my tenth book with Quadrille and it's been an absolute pleasure working with you. Thank you for all your support, creative input, guidance and shared enthusiasm to make this book come together.

Secondly, I want to thank my dedicated team, starting with my two very talented and passionate pastry chefs – head chef Alisée Lesobre and sous chef Emily Brook. I couldn't be prouder of you both and the edible works of art that you produce on a day-to-day basis. Your artistic and baking expertise has been invaluable in creating this book. From developing some of the most delicious recipes to fine-tuning, testing and documenting to ensure the recipes work in a domestic environment, your role has been pivotal. You are a formidable team and just as importantly, you are both a pleasure to work with.

A massive thank you goes to our floral designer Mathew Dickinson of Dickinson & Doris and his team. Mathew is one of the loveliest and most genuine people you'll ever know, and he plays an integral part in developing our seasonal themes and installations; he completely blows my mind time and time again. I'm so happy that we found each other again. Thank you for sharing my vision and contributing with your endless creativity, dedication and support over the years. You have truly helped shape the Parlour concept and it wouldn't be where it is today without you. Thank you for sharing your expert advice with us in this book! I'm so pleased to be able to give your work the credit it deserves and share your stunning installations with the rest of the world.

Another big thank you goes to our amazing photographer Paul Plews, whom I started working with by default back in 2015, after he was filling in for his then pregnant wife Sue. I feel fortunate to have found a photographer who connects with our brand, and who shares my passion for perfection, dedication and work ethic. You are one of the nicest and kindest people to work with and I have complete trust in you and what you do. You didn't know it then, but what started off with simple cutout photography evolved into something really special. I always felt that the images we created right from the start were the stuff of dreams that were made to go into a book. I hope that you are as proud as I am of what we have created together.

While expressing myself through my creations is the easy part, I find it more challenging to equally express myself through words. I have a huge admiration for creative writing; it's a unique skill that I wish I had. This is where I would like to thank the amazingly gifted Hannah Clifford, who has made a huge contribution to this book. Thank you for your wonderful talent for being able to not only translate but elevate my designs and collections into inspiring storytelling that takes us on an imaginary journey. It's not only your creative writing skills I cherish, but also your professional guidance and the confidence that you instill in me when I feel flustered and my creative mind is in need of focus. When I don't make sense to myself and get stuck for words, you manage to sum up my 'gibberish' in a way that makes complete sense and actually helps me to understand myself as a creative, a professional and as a human being. I love working with you and have learned so much from you along the way. I can't thank you enough for your amazing contribution in helping me write this book and tell the story of our journey. A journey that you have helped us shape and summarise into an inspiring story which has made this book even more special and something that I feel really proud of.

I would also like to make a special thank you to my in-house designer Kate Charlwood. You have played an enormous part in bringing the Parlour to life through your dexterous use of graphic design. Our natural synergy is so special to me, and I greatly admire your ability to weave your design magic throughout the many ways in which we

communicate about the brand. Thank you for always being so imaginative, diligent and quick!

A successful recipe book first and foremost needs to work for the people who read it. Scaling commercial size recipes down to make them suitable for domestic use and making sure they work can be tricky. I couldn't have done this without the help of my fantastic army of test-bakers whose shared enthusiasm and feedback have been invaluable. This is a special thank you to members of my family, colleagues, friends, and friends of friends for offering your time and baking experience to test some of the recipes in this book. A big thank you to my mother-in-law Georgie and her friend Carol, my sister-in-law Ella, Emma, Hannah and Leah, Charlene, Jovita and Silvia. I really appreciate you taking the time and effort in making this happen. And my dear mother-in-law Georgie who lives in New Zealand, even wrote a poem about her baking experience which I thought I'd share with you – see overleaf.

Carol & Georgie made a cake
It was so special, there could be no mistake
To be included in a new 'Coffee Table Book'
The taste was vital, along with a perfect look
Every ingredient weighed with precision
No deviation or alternative personal decision
Weighing egg whites must be tricky
Any spillage would be rather sticky
Unlimited patience was required
A perfect result was desired
An acknowledgement will surely come their way
As the author will surely thank them & say
'Well done Ladies for taking on the task
You have done all I could possibly ask.

There are so many people that have worked with us and left their mark by making a difference to the Peggy Porschen Parlour brand over the years. I would like to thank all of you for your input, hard work and dedication that has helped us to become who we are today. There is one person I would like to say a very special thank you to – my dear friend and former head chef Franziska Klausmann. It is thanks to you that I learned to understand who we are as a brand and where we should go with our retail concept. Together, you helped me create a new identity for our product and brand experience back in Christmas 2016, which we are still building on today. I cherish your passion, enthusiasm and continued support and guidance, creative chats and letting me bounce ideas off you still today. I hope that you feel proud to see in this book some of the recipes and designs you helped create during your time with us.

I would like to thank the wonderful customers, media friends and influencers, as well as our prized social media fans, who have been by our side over the years and helped us grow by sharing their love for what we do. There are too many to name, but I would like to mention: @victoriametaxas and @therollinsonlondon, you were two of the first to discover our magic and spread the Parlour around the world with your beautiful images and storytelling. Victoria, your wonderful images of the Parlour over the years have provided the perfect backdrop to support the lifestyle thread within this book, and I am especially proud of the iconic Summer 2017 Parlour shot that you captured so magically all that time ago; @prettycitylondon for your authentic photography and featuring the Parlour at its prettiest, and for including us in your beautiful books, which put us firmly on the 'pretty city London' map; fellow author @georgiannalane for making me so proud by featuring the Belgravia Parlour as the 'cover girl' of your beautiful book *London in Bloom* – this truly captured the dreaminess of our location; @wanderforawhile for the pure joy you bring through your styling and photography and for being so supportive; @gulshanlondon and @galinathomas for bringing style and elegance to the Parlour; @hellomissjordan for adding a touch of dazzling magic to every new season. A special thank you also to Cally Squires, Editor @belgraviamagazine for championing us so eloquently within our local area. And also to Mena @onjenu and Farley @ladyberrycupcakes, among many others, for your endless support in spotlighting female business owners. Also @eatnlondon, @ritafarhifinds, @londoncoffeeshops, @bei.bei.wei, @freyasfairytale, @catherine.mw, @sophiesierra_, @emmasallyh, @ananewyork and so many more. Thank you all for always being so supportive and for everything you have done. I encourage readers of this book to follow all of these inspiring women on Instagram.

To my family in Germany, for being by my side from a distance and sharing all the ups and downs this past year has brought. Thank you for always thinking of me, guiding me and keeping me grounded throughout. And for your never-ending love and support.

Last but not least, my biggest heartfelt thank you goes to my two amazing boys – my husband and business partner Bryn and my seven-year-old son Max. Writing this book during the 2020 lockdown and ongoing Covid pandemic has been challenging, and added extra pressure on family life during an already unprecedented situation. Thank you for giving me the time and space that I needed to produce this book. Being able to focus on a new project when everything else seemed to stand still has helped me focus and given me something to look forward to whilst the hospitality industry has suffered. It would not have been possible without your patience and understanding. I hope that I make you as proud as you make me. This book is for you; I love you so much!

Published in 2021 by Quadrille,
an imprint of Hardie Grant Publishing

Quadrille
52–54 Southwark Street
London SE1 1UN
quadrille.com

Publishing Director – Sarah Lavelle
Senior Commissioning Editor – Céline Hughes
Designer – Alicia House
Food Stylist and Prop Stylist – Peggy Porschen
Photographer – Paul Plews, except photographs on pages 6,
79 (top right), 83, 104 (top right) 119 and 189 – Victoria Metaxas
Production Controller – Nikolaus Ginelli
Head of Production – Stephen Lang

Cataloguing in Publication Data: a catalogue record for this book is available
from the British Library.

ISBN 9781787136861

Printed in China